D1568284

The Essays Only You Can Write

The Essays Only You Can Write

IRENE PAPOULIS

broadview press

BROADVIEW PRESS – www.broadviewpress.com
Peterborough, Ontario, Canada

Founded in 1985, Broadview Press remains a wholly independent publishing house. Broadview's focus is on academic publishing; our titles are accessible to university and college students as well as scholars and general readers. With over 800 titles in print, Broadview has become a leading international publisher in the humanities, with world-wide distribution. Broadview is committed to environmentally responsible publishing and fair business practices.

Library and Archives Canada Cataloguing in Publication

Title: The essays only you can write / Irene Papoulis.
Names: Papoulis, Irene, 1954- author.
Description: Includes bibliographical references and index.
Identifiers: Canadiana (print) 20230538363 | Canadiana (ebook) 20230538401 | ISBN 9781554815760 (softcover) | ISBN 9781770489233 (PDF) | ISBN 9781460408544 (EPUB)
Subjects: LCSH: Academic writing—Study and teaching. | LCSH: Essay—Authorship.
Classification: LCC P301.5.A27 P37 2023 | DDC 808.02—dc23

Broadview Press handles its own distribution in North America:
PO Box 1243, Peterborough, Ontario K9J 7H5, Canada
555 Riverwalk Parkway, Tonawanda, NY 14150, USA
Tel: (705) 743-8990; Fax: (705) 743-8353
email: customerservice@broadviewpress.com

For all territories outside of North America, distribution is handled by Eurospan Group.

Canada Broadview Press acknowledges the financial support of the Government of Canada for our publishing activities.

Edited by Tania Therien
Book Design by Em Dash Design

PRINTED IN CANADA

Contents

Acknowledgements   7

Preface for Students   9

Introduction: Starting Ideas and Fundamental Practices   11

PART ONE / Writing a Personal Essay   33

Chapter 1:   Get to Know the Personal Essay as a Genre and Move towards Your Own   34

Chapter 2:   Find a Way to Structure and Compose Your Personal Essay   48

Chapter 3:   Get Feedback on Your Draft and Revise It   64

PART TWO / Writing an Essay about a Text   81

Chapter 4:   On Reading and Writing about Texts   82

Chapter 5:   Read and Respond to Your Assigned Text   96

Chapter 6:   Write Your Essay about a Text   100

Chapter 7:   Learn from Other Writers as You Revise Your Draft   116

PART THREE / Writing a Research Essay   123

Chapter 8:   Confront Your Research Assignment   124

Chapter 9:   Do Your Research   134

Chapter 10: Write Your Research Essay   142

Chapter 11: Get Feedback on Your Draft and Revise It   154

PART FOUR / Mindfulness and Essay Writing   157

Chapter 12: Introductory Thoughts on Mindfulness   158

Chapter 13: The Psychology of Writing   170

PART FIVE / Giving and Receiving Feedback in Peer Groups   181

Chapter 14: The Psychology of Feedback   182

Chapter 15: Being a Peer Responder   192

Works Cited   207

Image Credits   209

Index   213

Acknowledgements

This book would not exist without Peter Elbow, mentor and dear friend. I was lucky to be galvanized early in my career by the power of his ideas; their ripples—this book is one—extend forever within our profession and beyond.

I am ever grateful to each of my students; you all taught me how to teach.

Much that informs this book grew out of countless meetings, collaborative writings, workshops, and communal plannings at the Institute for Writing and Thinking (IWT) at Bard College. I have been challenged and supported there by Mary Leonard, Sharon Marshall, Paul Connolly, Teresa Vilardi, Emily Miller Mlcak, Alfie Guy, Rob Whittemore, Michael Murray, Myra McLarey, Judy Miller, Pat Sharpe, Jamie Hutchinson, Glynis Benbow-Niemier, Jeff Berger-White, Erica Kaufman, Becca Chase, Celia Bland, Michelle Hoffman, Madhu Kaza, Alice Lesnick, Darlene Forrest, Nicole Wallack, Eléna Rivera, Carley Moore, William Webb, Jim Keller, Ric Campbell, Anna Dolan, Sean Mills, and every other IWT associate I've encountered. I also thank all the amazing teachers who attended IWT workshops, on campus and beyond.

I am also lucky to have enjoyed productive conversations with many Trinity College colleagues and other delightful friends and family, among them Jane Danielewicz, Wendy Ryden, Marilyn Zucker, Jackie Cossentino, Diana Paulin, Robert Vestigo, Richard Williams, Sheridan Blau, Don Jones, Carl and Stella Herzig, Dennis and Janet Clarke, Satsie Veith, Lori Cohen, Jeanne Costello, Stan Scott, Libby Falk Jones, Joonna Trapp, Wilma Romatz, Nate Mickelson, Bruce Novak, Jonathan Budd, Lorri Chapman, Jean Martin, Elizabeth Keifer, Helen Papoulis, Jim Papoulis, Ann Papoulis, Mary Papoulis, Cyrus Duff, Michael O. Duff, Beverly Wall, Becca Tarsa, Robert Peltier, Cindy Butos, Wendy Graveley, Tennyson O'Donnell, Nicholas Marino, Erin Frymire, Alex Helberg, Dan Mrozowski, James Truman, Lucy Ferriss, and

Tanetta Andersson. Ethan Rutherford's question after a faculty workshop, "Is any of this written down?" was the catalyst for this book.

Long ago, at my first teaching job at the University of California, Santa Barbara, I had the pleasure of participating in the South Coast chapter of the National Writing Project. Thanks to Sheridan Blau's leadership, I had many life-changing experiences there, including writing, and sharing writing, regularly in large groups—a practice that has enhanced my teaching ever since. Along with many exhilarating readings in our Writing Project's summer institute I learned of James Moffett's work; his ideas on mindfulness and writing planted seeds in me that were only cultivated many years later. My experiences with NCTE's Association for Expanded Perspectives on Learning were fruitful as well.

I thank Luis Figueroa-Martínez, wonderful partner in endless ways, for enhancing this book at every step with his beautiful love, understanding, feedback, and patience.

I am also grateful for the incisiveness and generosity of my dream team of editors at Broadview Press—Brett McLenithan, Tania Therien, and Tara Lowes.

Preface for Students

Dear Students,

All writing is personal. Even if the essays you write have nothing to do with your life, your written words reveal something about you.

That may be scary, but it is exciting too; communicating your own truths in a clear way can be satisfying and even fun.

But in a time when experts in artificial intelligence are training computers to write "essays," you might ask, why should we humans continue to write them?

The answer lies in the vastness and beauty of *human* intelligence. Essays written by computers are laughably empty. They may provide usable information, and you might find it useful to explore how they work. But the essays you'll learn to write in this book could *never* be written by a computer. Only *you* can write essays that grow out of your own lived experiences and thoughts.

Becoming proficient at the skills of essay writing is an excellent way to develop your sophistication as an academic thinker and communicator. Essays of all sorts are an invaluable form of expression, both as art and as a means of public and academic discourse. When you drink in someone else's essay your mind is nourished, and when you write your own you go on a journey into the many layers of your own thinking.

Maybe you have already had the pleasure of writing essays you are proud of and sharing them with others. Or perhaps you habitually fret about your writing, dislike doing it, and worry whether you have interesting or valid things to say.

Wherever you are with writing, this book will help you get better.

In the first three parts I'll be leading you through three main essay assignments: a personal essay, an essay about readings, and a research essay. Each will take a total of four weeks, during which you will explore each essay's form and then write, read, reflect, draft, and revise. I'll encourage you to develop and trust your own thinking as you learn skills and strategies for writing essays that only you can write, in response to your professors' assignments. The information and experience you get from this book will be useful both for the class you're currently in and for essays you'll write for the rest of your life.

The last two parts of the book are for you to read at any point in the course. Part Four is about mindfulness and how it can help you with psychological and practical issues that may arise while writing. Part Five is about feedback, with specific guidance for working in groups with classmates and other peers.

Happy writing!

Starting Ideas and Fundamental Practices

EXERCISE 1
Your Writing Process So Far

Answer the first question below and then three or four of the subsequent questions. Write down your answers first and then share them in conversation with one or more classmates. As you listen to your peers, note the differences and similarities among you:

- Do you like writing? Why or why not?
- What is your favorite kind of essay to write? Least favorite?
- When you write essays for school, do you write them just once, or revise them?
- Is your process of writing different depending on the kind of assignment you have? How?
- What is your favorite part of the process of writing an essay? Least favorite?
- Is there anything about writing essays that you wish you could learn to do differently?

First of All, What Is an Essay?

Many students come to college thinking that writing an **essay** is a single type of writing project, whether you write it for a literature class, a history seminar, a psychology exam, or in any other context. But that's not the case.

Just as films are divided into genres of comedy, drama, thriller, etc., essays are divided by genre as well. Your essay assignments in college will most likely involve genres ranging from argumentative essays to book reviews, close readings of texts, philosophical meditations, interviews, summaries, research reports, and many other genres your professors might assign. From one academic discipline to another, and even within one college class, your assignments will require you to write essays in very different ways.

Some genres, from lab reports to legal briefs, have strict rules of form and content that writers must follow; others give you more freedom to write in a way that suits you. But behind the scenes of *any* genre there's an author working to articulate something that hasn't been said before, using practices that fit the genre's purpose. As you'll see in this book, you can bring your own personal spark to your work within the conventions of any genre you write in. Even if it's an often-used genre, on a topic many others have also written about, no one has written the words *you* will write as you construct your essays.

"Genre"

An essay's **genre** is its "type," or "style," or "subject." For example, an **argumentative** essay is a genre in which the writer takes a position and demonstrates its truth with evidence; an **analysis** can be defined as one that explores various elements of a topic.

There are many genres of essays in the academic world and beyond, and each has its own conventions and rules. Writing effective essays requires that you are aware of the genre you're writing in, and what its audience expects from you. Read essays in the genres you write in and ask professors about how they work.

In a sense, all essays are "personal," since they are based on the writer's particular way of looking at and engaging with a topic. But there's a big difference between personal in the sense of "I'll tell you about my life" and personal in the sense of "here's how I think about this topic."

Even in **personal essays**, the genre you'll explore in Part One of this book, there is plenty of variation. Many personal essays explore an author's lived experience in autobiographical detail. But a "meditation" is a personal essay in which the writer reflects on a question or idea, describing how their mind moves to consider various sides of it. You wouldn't necessarily know about the writer's *life* from that sort of essay, though you would still get an idea of who the writer is as a person.

When you read **academic essays**, in contrast, you're probably much more interested in ideas and information than in who the writer is. And yet academics make many individual choices in writing such essays: what to emphasize, how to describe things, what kind of voice to use, and which directions to pursue. Such decisions give you a sense of the writer as a person, even if you know nothing about their lived experience.

Creating essays in *any* genre requires you to make choices that reflect something about your uniqueness.

"Voice"

A writer's voice is the "sound" of their language. Even when you read quietly to yourself, you get a sense of a writer by the way they "speak" to you. Different genres require different voices: a personal essay can be informal and chatty; a psychology case study should sound scholarly and serious.

To communicate well in our culture you need fluency in a range of media, not just the written word, so learning to write can also involve learning to use that media effectively. I'll be instructing you here solely in written forms, but I hope and expect that you can apply the ideas and methods in this book to creating expository work in all media. It is possible to view films, webpages, podcasts, and other electronic media as electronic forms of essays, in that they work by leading viewers or listeners through a constructed series of concepts made coherent by an overarching theme and structure.

So how does the process of creating an essay work? Some students come to college or university imagining that professional writers compose essays and books by starting with the first sentence, writing paragraph by paragraph through to the end, and then sitting back with satisfaction, finished.

However, good writing of any kind virtually never works like that.

Writing means revising, and revising means far more than adding a sentence or two to a first draft and making a few grammatical changes. The process of constructing an essay works at its best when it involves drafting in various stages, and then sharing, deleting, adding, sharing some more, adding more, deleting more, reshaping, sharing, rethinking, adding, deleting, sharing, and doing it all over again—not necessarily in that order or that number of times, but you get the idea.

As you revise, keep your audience in mind. What do they expect from the genre you're writing in? What will they value? The more you know about the type of essay you are writing, the easier it will be to answer those questions.

Your essays should start out one way and become quite different once you've revised them. Maybe you've heard about the idea attributed to the artist Michelangelo talking about his sculpture: that the beautiful statues he made were *already there* in the blocks of marble he started with—he simply had to chisel the rock away to get to them. Chiseling takes a long time, and sometimes revising can feel the same way: the rough draft is the rough marble, unfinished, and the process of hacking at, shaping and re-thinking, allows you to discover the essay that's been lurking there, the essay only you can write, even though at first you didn't know what its shape should be, or how you would fill in its details.

Two Muscles: Creative and Critical

Theorist Peter Elbow wrote about the fact that writing involves two different skills or "mentalities": the creative and the critical (7). I like to view them as "muscles." The **creative muscle** works as we *draft* essays: it helps us explore. The **critical muscle** is responsible for *revising*: it helps us shape our creative muscle's ideas into a coherent essay.

Composing an essay does not require each muscle to work only once, with the creative muscle writing the draft, the critical muscle revising it, and then the essay is ready to go. Once an essay draft is underway, the two muscles are at their best when they find a rhythm of alternating back and forth.

Some writers tend to be better at using their creative muscle. They're the ones who write endless pages of journal entries and emails that go on longer than average. Others are more comfortable on the critical side—their strength is to shape an essay's clarity. How about you? Are you more comfortable with one or the other?

Wherever your comfort zone is, the process of writing a good essay demands that you are adept with both muscles. However, when writers try to use both muscles at the same time, they can get stuck. Each muscle needs space to work on its own.

Your creative muscle needs space and time to create: if your critical muscle jumps in too soon with advice about what's bad, what's good, and how you should change things, it can stifle your creative muscle with doubts that freeze the flow of ideas.

The critical muscle needs time to shape and revise: if your creative muscle gets impatient with the details of revision and insists on endless new beginnings, the result can be that the essay never gets done.

Imbalance between the two muscles, in other words, can be counterproductive.

My goal is to help you develop a great relationship with both your creative and your critical muscles, so they can work in harmony to shape your insights and knowledge into excellent essays. The key is to let each muscle work *at the right time* in the process of writing all types of essays.

Your Creative Muscle: How It Works and How to Work It

We all have deep wells of creative ideas. There's mystery in the fact that while those ideas emerge from within us, our conscious minds can't necessarily control or determine in advance what they will be. Whether we're writing a poem or solving a mathematical equation, new insights show up from "somewhere" and surprise us. The more open we are to them the more regularly they will come forth.

How can we tone our "creative muscle," teaching it to become better at taking us beyond our more superficial insights and into the sources of creative ideas? In *theory*, the answer is easy: all we need to do is let our ideas flow!

Easier said than done though, right? "Let your creative ideas flow" might sound simple, but it can also seem impossible. We might not know what to say or write, or we might think we need more information before generating useful thoughts. Or a chorus of criticism inside our heads might tell us that we *can't* come up with new ideas.

As a student, you develop your ideas through learning and questioning. But as you do so it's important to explore the quirks of your own thinking that you might not even have known you had. **Freewriting** is a practice that can help you get in touch with your creative ideas and let them flow.

What Is Freewriting?

It is writing without stopping, encouraging ideas to move out from your head to your page or screen. In its purest form, freewriting doesn't have to be, or be ready to become, anything formal or finished. It doesn't have to be "creative," in the sense of beautiful or artistic. Instead, it's a way to work your creative muscle like physical conditioning works for athletes: they must exercise so they can play the game well, but the exercise itself is not the game.

If *the game* is the finished essay, freewriting is the *practice* of exercising the muscle that will get you to generate effective writing once it's time to play the game of getting to your final draft. It can be a painless way to grab ideas from the never-ending perceptions that are always boiling within you, sometimes beyond your conscious awareness.

There are various types of freewriting, as you'll see throughout this book. We'll begin with its purest form, unattached to any specific writing project: *writing nonstop, without thinking in advance about what you will write.*

Of course, whatever is in your head is not necessarily something you want anyone else to know about. It's nobody's business! I agree—in fact, this exercise only works if it is private, between you and yourself. You're welcome to delete what you write or rip it into pieces as soon as you're done, because the goal is simply the *process*. The *content* of what you write doesn't matter right now, because we just want to exercise your creative muscle, encouraging it to get words, any words, from your head to the page.

EXERCISE 2 (IN 2 STEPS)
Exercise Your Creative Muscle by Freewriting

Step One

This exercise requires no preparation except a pen and paper or new document on your screen. It is *private*: you don't have to show this writing to anyone. Read through these directions before you begin:

- Set a timer for five minutes.
- Start writing and don't stop. Write in sentences or phrases, not bullet points, as though you are talking onto the page.
- If you don't think you have anything to say, write a phrase like, "I am stuck." If you like, write a question to yourself about it, for example, "Why am I stuck?" Write an answer, or write about anything else, and keep going. If you get stuck again, write about that, or repeat words. The goal here is not to produce finished writing, it's to force your creative muscle to keep accessing and recording whatever happens to be in your head right now. There is always *something* there.
- You don't have to worry about grammar or sticking to a point; simply follow whatever ideas come to you.
- Follow your writing wherever it goes. Don't worry if it keeps changing direction and comes out looking like a "mess." You can delete it when it's done or throw it in the recycling bin, knowing you have *exercised your creative muscle* to get it in good shape for essay writing.

STUDENT EXAMPLE
An Example of Student Freewriting

I'm not sure what I'm thinking this isn't working I like her shoes I am feeling uncomfortable what do I really have to say I don't know I don't know. I'm tired I should have gone to bed earlier why did I sign up for this 9am class, I will never be a morning person, besides it's fun to stay up late and also how could I sleep everyone was running back and forth until 2am. Jody never seems to study but who knows she seems to do well in classes. When is this going to be over? I am not writing anything useful I'm stuck I'm stuck what's for lunch, what's in my head the class would be better if it were later in the day. What does this writing have to do with writing essays I don't know I don't know I am tired and don't know what I'm thinking she said not to bore yourself but what if my own thinking is boring me.

EXERCISE 2 (CONTINUED)
Exercise Your Creative Muscle by Freewriting

Step Two

With a peer, your class, or just yourself, reflect on how the process of freewriting worked for you.

- How did you feel while doing this writing?
- Without going into specifics about what you wrote, what did you notice about how you proceeded—did you stay on the same subject? Did you switch gears often? Did you get frustrated? What else did you notice about how the words went, or didn't go, from your head to the page?

A potential obstacle to freewriting is the worry about what it looks like, even if we know no one but us will read it. Odd, isn't it? We may feel self-conscious *in front of ourselves*. If you don't like the way your freewriting looks and you're prone to blaming yourself, you might think, "I'm just no good at freewriting." Or, if you are prone to blaming others, you might say, "Freewriting is clearly a useless activity that doesn't work!"

I encourage you to let such responses go and simply accept your freewriting, however it turns out. People who are out of shape don't look smooth and effective when they begin a conditioning run, but that's certainly not a reason to stop! The "nonsense" that might emerge in your freewrites is the writing-equivalent of physical muscles warming up. Keep going. You're establishing a practice of fluency that will eventually allow you better access to your own ideas.

Your creative muscle's primary job is to find and dig into new material. Restarting it might hurt, just as physical muscles hurt when you use them again after disuse. Since it's a muscle, albeit a figurative one, your creative muscle can atrophy if it isn't nurtured enough. Freewriting on a regular basis can keep it in shape.

Be wary of your inner critic, who might say things like

- "That's not good."
- "That *is* good."
- "Change that."
- "That doesn't make any sense."
- "You started out okay but you're going nowhere."

Such thoughts may be useful when you revise, but they can make your creative muscle spasm and freeze when you're freewriting. Remember, it's supposed to be "free"! Do your best to banish your own judgments at this stage. There will be time later to get in touch with your critical side.

People who have the most trouble with freewriting are often those who need it most. They often don't realize that voices in their heads are holding down their creative muscle, preventing it from finding its best ideas. Taking time to jumpstart the flow of creativity by writing without stopping can really help.

Focused Freewriting

To exercise your creative muscle, you can use private freewriting as a study break, or even just to explore why something bothers you.

There's also a more direct way to use freewriting when it comes to writing essays: **focused freewriting**. As its name suggests, focused freewriting is informal and unstructured, but meant to flesh out ideas on a *specific topic*. Here's how to do it:

- Begin with an "exploratory" topic: "What in my past could I write a memoir-essay about?" for example, or "What are my thoughts on that question my teacher has assigned for my essay?" etc. Without planning, begin writing about your topic.
- Follow tangents that come up, but keep circling back to your topic, perhaps by including questions to yourself as you write, such as, "What does this add to my thoughts about the topic?" Or "Is there an angle on the topic that I haven't gotten to?" Or "Why is this topic leading me in *that* direction?"

- When your stream of ideas slows down, keep going at least a bit longer: You might turn your last sentence into a question, answer it, and see where the answer takes you.

The point of focused freewriting is to use your creative muscle to explore a range of ideas about your topic. Most of the creative-muscle exercises in this book involve this second type of freewriting, which will help you gather material for your formal essays.

Here are some ways you can use focused freewriting:

To respond to readings: Useful when you need to keep a record of how you reacted to passages from your readings, to set you up for writing about the readings later (see also Part Two).

To get your emotions out: Useful when you are distracted by something while you're doing other work. Write to yourself about how you feel! In addition to exercising your creative muscle, it can be a great way to help you put emotions aside temporarily while you get your work done.

To figure out a problem or dilemma you encounter in the middle of writing an essay: Useful when you think, while writing, "oh no—this idea I'm arriving at contradicts what I was just saying on the previous page!" Exploring that contradiction in a separate freewrite can help you deepen the ideas in your essay, for example by using the contradiction as part of your thesis.

To find ideas you didn't yet know you had: Useful when you know you want to write about something, and you even might sense that it is a powerful topic for you, but you're not yet sure exactly what you want to say about it. Just start writing, and don't stop for a while—you might surprise yourself.

To learn about your own writing process: Useful when you want to learn more about what works for you as a writer, and what parts of your process you'd like to change. While you are writing something, or immediately after, stop to ask yourself, "How did I feel when I wrote that? Why?" You can learn a lot by talking about your writing experience with others, and hearing about theirs. For example, here is a focused freewrite by a student who was frustrated by his process:

STUDENT EXAMPLE
A Student's Focused Freewrite about His Frustration with an Essay He Wrote

I am someone that enjoys writing because it gets me to be able explore different thoughts in my brain ... Though I enjoy writing, it is something that I have always had a difficult time with. This is because I am one who struggles to extend the ideas that I have. Often when I do try I feel as though I sound repetitive and I don't want to bore the reader. This caused that essay I wrote on the Tulsa Massacre to fall short of its full potential. Most of the time I have a very great idea that I will write about, however according to the feedback that I heard from the people that read my writing, I make an exciting or interesting point but I fail to extend it. This failure will often have the reader feeling disappointed or as though I had wasted a very good idea, which is what happened. (JS)

After writing this, the student began to explore ways to extend his ideas with focused freewrites.

EXERCISE 3 (IN 2 STEPS)
Explore Your Writing Process

Step One: A Focused Freewrite about Something You've Written

Think of something you've written in the past—an essay, story, poem, play, lab report, or anything else. It can be something you wrote either for school or outside of school. You might start by making a list of past writings and then choose one. *Your topic is your experience with that one piece of writing.*

- Begin writing about your experience from any angle that comes to mind first. Here are a few possible starting points:
  - » Was your writing assigned? Who assigned it? How did you feel about the assignment? If it wasn't assigned, what made you write it?
  - » What moment in the writing process is the clearest to you as you think back?
  - » Who, if anyone, read your writing?
  - » What feelings did you have about the writing and any responses you got to it? Do you see them differently now?

- Keep freewriting for about ten minutes. Follow tangents if they arise, but keep circling back to the topic of your writing experience. Here are more questions you might address:
  - » What steps did you take as you wrote?
  - » Do you have any regrets about your experience?
  - » What are you most proud of?

Step Two: Process Writing: What Was That Like for You?

Before sharing your focused freewrite with peers or your professor, take some time to reflect on writing it:

- What thoughts were in your mind as you wrote?
- What was your process of making use of the various questions—did you stick with one? Ignore them all? Keep picking and choosing?
- Did anything surprise you in your process of writing?
- What do you notice now as you read over what you wrote?
- Is there a part you especially like or dislike?

After doing this exercise, you will have an idea of how focused freewriting works. Maybe you enjoyed it and love what you wrote, or maybe you struggled. Either way, keep going. Freewriting is different each time you do it.

Freewrite Clarification 1: It Is Not Busywork!

Students sometimes get the mistaken idea that freewriting is only something to do "on the side," unconnected to the "real" process of drafting an actual essay. "Freewrite about these ideas for a while to brainstorm," a teacher might have told those students in the past, "and then put your freewrites aside and begin writing your draft."

That might work, in theory. But it could also lead pragmatic students to say, "How about if I just skip the freewriting part and start with the draft; it saves time!"

Yes, you *could* write an essay simply by starting with your introduction and building the structure of your essay from there. You might have done so in the past. "Start with an outline," many professors have said and still say, "in which you make use of established structures or formulas." Those formulas might include the "five-paragraph essay," with an introduction stating a thesis, three examples of the thesis, and a conclusion; a "comparison/contrast essay" in which the first two paragraphs point to similarities between two things and the second two explore differences; or many other fixed forms.

Such formulas can be useful at times. But in my experience, students who use them with an "outline first and then write" process tend to write essays that are pinched and dull, not interesting to the writer, much less the reader. Why bother?

In contrast, learning to *incorporate freewriting into your drafting process* helps to wake up your creativity and get you far more engaged. However, that leads me to my second clarification about freewriting.

Freewrite Clarification 2: It Is Not the Essay!

Students are often surprised that once they start freewriting on a topic, they generate even more pages of freewriting than the page length required in their essay assignment. Their excitement about that can lead them to think that once they have the right number of freewritten pages they have completed an interesting essay. It's certainly interesting to them! So they turn it in as a draft.

My job at that point is to disappoint them. While their freewritten "essay" contains great *potential*, and may even be engaging to read, it is not an essay yet. It needs a critical muscle to nurture, shape, and structure it! Reading raw freewriting is like reading someone's diary—if it's written by a person you love or are super-curious about it might contain fascinating moments for you, but even then it can get old fast because it will likely be rambling, repetitive, or otherwise ineffective. It's like someone rolling out of bed in their pajamas and going straight to a fancy party—they need to take time to get dressed up! Your raw writing always needs dressing up to become properly presentable to the reader. As a freewrite, it's only halfway there.

Essays require much more than freewrites do. You insult the reader if you expect them to pore through your freewrites looking for gems of insights. Your job is to find those gems yourself and make them work in a systematic and satisfying way.

This might sound like a lot of work. But don't despair! As I'll explain, the process of "building" your essay can be much easier, fun, and rewarding when you become adept at weaving freewriting into your process. Freewrites certainly do give you plenty of useful material—in fact, as you'll see, sometimes you can lift whole sections out of them to deposit into parts of your essay drafts.

An Aside: More Thoughts about Voice in Writing

If you know someone well, you probably recognize their voice as soon as they say one word. You might have had the same experience while reading, too, when a few sentences signal a familiar writer's "voice."

Different types of essays contain different voices. Formal, serious, academic, meditative, angry, confessional, funny—there are endless possibilities. Even when a writer writes in many different styles, a close read would probably reveal elements that signal that writer's particular "voice."

It is hard to define exactly what makes a writer's voice unique, but like spoken voice it has to do with the rhythm of language and sentences, and even the choices of topics, words, and approaches.

As you develop as a writer, your own "writing voice" will develop too.

One important rule for writing is that within any single essay it is important to have a *consistent* voice. Experienced writers might combine voices in a way that suits their essay's purpose, but if you shift for no reason between, say, a serious academic tone and an emotional one your essay will seem unnecessarily confused.

The best way to get a feel for how the voice in your own writing works is to read it aloud, even to yourself alone in your room.

Your Critical Muscle: Its Job Is to Revise

When you freewrite, your critical muscle's job is to stand back and keep quiet. But when it's time to shape your raw material into coherent essays, your critical muscle gets its turn to shine.

Your critical muscle represents your logical, analytic side. It can work with the raw material of your freewrites and figure out how to shape their ideas into a clear essay. That involves being able to conceive of your essay as a whole, answering questions like, "What is the genre and purpose of this essay?" "What kind of voice does this essay have?" "Which ideas are most important?" "What order should they go in?" "What sections should be added or deleted?" and many other tasks, from rethinking decisions, to making sure your voice is consistent, to checking grammar and spelling, etc.

The critical muscle usually starts the process by understanding what kind of an essay you are writing, and then developing a structure and plan that will work. There's no one way to do that, and as you'll see in this book, each essay you write requires a different kind of effort from your critical muscle.

Perfectionism, Secret Perfectionism, and How a Writer's Psychology Might Get in the Way

Before we move toward drafting your first mini-essay I want to say a bit more about psychology, in case you might get stuck at any point in the drafting and revising process with a terrible feeling of "this isn't working, I can't write this."

It could be that what you need at that point is to talk with your professor or a writing tutor about the material of your essay, and I urge you to do so.

A common reason for that frustrated-with-writing feeling is that the judge inside your head is too harsh with you. It might tell you that your idea makes no sense, that you'll never be a good writer, or any other useless criticism it comes up with that might get you to dismiss the seeds of your ideas before they even get a chance to grow into an interesting plant. Even if you know that those inner judgments are wrong and don't serve you well, *it isn't so easy to stop them.*

When I first assign freewriting, some students happily begin writing to the prompts right away. Others, though, think for a long time, begin writing, and then almost immediately put their pens down, frowning. They cross out what they wrote, write a few more words, and then cross things out again. They write another word or two and look out the window. If I say, "Keep going; write anything in your head," they grudgingly reread their writing, cross out even more, and begin again, but soon stop and glance at the clock, willing the class to be over.

Such students might seem unengaged, and sometimes they are. But their stuckness can also be a sign that they are trying *too hard*, as opposed to *not hard enough*. They might be trying to write something "perfect" and criticizing themselves for any less-than-beautiful sentence. You have probably heard the advice such students often hear: "just loosen up!"

If you can't loosen up when you're writing, it's most likely because your critical muscle isn't giving your creative muscle enough of a chance. Imagine a child running happily to a friend or teacher to share a new idea. If the response is, "no, that doesn't make any sense! It's a terrible idea. Find something better," they may wilt, become irritable, and maybe keep their next idea to themselves. If that process happens repeatedly, they might stop even knowing what their ideas are.

That kind of unfortunate encounter can happen quite regularly *inside our heads* as we write, even if we're not aware of it. As a child gets older, their stern teacher or parent can transform into a voice inside them, made up of all the critical judgments they've heard about their writing or themselves. "Too choppy," "too bland," "not structured enough," "undeveloped," "disorganized," "boring," "not grammatically correct," etc. The psychological effects of comments like that can last a lifetime.

Writers might see criticism of a single piece of writing as not just about that piece but about *who they are*: "I *am* a poor writer," or "I *am* bad at descriptions," or "I *am* too wordy," as though those qualities are fixed and impossible to change. They aren't! Those qualities in fact can always be changed.

If you judge yourself relentlessly, you might be a "perfectionist," or you might even be what I call a *secret perfectionist*. I once met a tennis coach at a party who asked if I played. "Uh, a little," I said, "but I'm terrible, and haven't really gotten anywhere." "Oh," he said, "you must be a perfectionist." What? Me? I was surprised, since I was nothing like what I imagined a tennis perfectionist to be: someone who'd patiently practice serves and volleys for hours until they got it right. I certainly didn't see my feeble attempts at tennis games as perfectionistic at all. I just felt bad because I wasn't any good.

But the coach explained that in his experience, sometimes people are such perfectionists that they can't stand to play tennis if they make a lot of mistakes at first. He'd seen lots of people walk away from the sport simply because they wouldn't allow themselves to be the beginners that they were.

Something clicked for me when he said that. Had I unconsciously *chosen not to play* rather than having to deal with the embarrassing realities of my imperfections as a tennis player? It sounded quite possible.

That kind of struggle applies to writers too: the desire to quit or do the minimum when it comes to writing can indicate that you want so much to be a fantastic writer that you can't bear to live with yourself as not-so-good. That fact can be a secret, even to yourself! Of course, the only way to become good at tennis, writing, or anything else is to keep going, knowing that the more you practice the better you become. But that's not easy when psychological forces are in your way.

It might be useful to know that even very successful writers have those unpleasant moments when their writing seems impossible to repair. They find ways of navigating those moments, and you can too. It's not easy to conquer harsh inner voices criticizing our writing. But becoming aware of them is an important first step, as is realizing that being "good" as a writer is something you really want. You'll find more tips about how mindfulness can help you in Part Four of this book.

Self-judgment isn't necessarily bad, of course. In fact, having a well-developed internal critic of your writing, one who insists that you revise until an essay really shines, is crucial if you want to produce really good writing. *We really need that critic* to help us make our essays, or our tennis playing, as good as they can be.

But that critic usually only works well when it stays away from useless and false criticisms that don't help, like, "you're a terrible writer" or "this will never work." A good internal critic leaves you alone in the early stages of a project, freeing you to stumble and make mistakes. Like athletes and musicians, we get better if we take plenty of time to *practice*, which in essay-writing can mean letting the creative muscle branch out at first, without being judged.

EXERCISE 4
Reflect on Your Inner Critical Voices

- What have you heard from teachers or other people about your writing, positive or negative?
- Do you have a voice in your head criticizing your writing?
- If so, what does it say, and how do you react?

Not all resistances to writing are based on inner psychological struggles, though. Sometimes the problem is that you simply are not sure how to proceed when you write, because you need answers to practical questions about how to generate ideas and structure them effectively.

The main essay assignments in the first three parts of this book will help you with that. Each focuses on a particular type of essay, and then leads you through composing one of your own. You'll use versions of the same moves you followed when you wrote your mini-essay: freewrite with your creative muscle to generate ideas, plan and shape those ideas with your critical muscle's assessments, and let the muscles take turns as you build the essay's content and structure.

MAIN ASSIGNMENT

Write a Mini-Essay in Two Parts

The purpose of this assignment is to help you discover some ways that your critical muscle can help you revise your creative muscle's creations. You'll use both muscles to construct *an informal mini-essay* (about 150–300 words).

Informal means that you can write in a conversational voice, without necessarily beginning with a formal introduction or ending with a fixed conclusion. However, your final version should contain at least two coherent paragraphs that allow the reader to follow your line of thinking.

PART **1**: YOUR LIST AND YOUR CHOICE

Follow this sequence of steps:

- Off the top of your head, *make a list of things you like*. Choose anything that comes to mind. For example, my list right now contains raspberries, swimming, giraffes, the color blue, my friend Luis, and city streets. What comes to mind for you?
- When you have at least five items, pause to look over your list. *Choose one item* you feel like spending some time with.
- *Do a focused freewrite* about that item for at least five minutes, seeing where your topic pulls you. Begin with whatever first thoughts on the item emerge when you start writing and keep going as other thoughts and stories arise. If you get stuck, ask yourself "what else?" and keep

writing: *you might comment on what you've written so far, ask a question, or delve into a specific memory.*

STUDENT EXAMPLE

From a Student's Focused Freewrite about Frogs

....

Frogs. What do I know about frogs? Not a bloody thing. They have warts, are slimy, they pee in your hand. Frogs croak, toads peep. Is that right? Are toads and frogs different? Frogs are amphibians. They like swampy areas, begin as tadpoles. Princesses kiss frogs and they change to princes. This is stupid. I know as much about frogs as I do about rockets.

Some frogs are poisonous and colorful. I remember a fairy tale about frogs where the princess kisses the frog and it turns into a prince. Or is it the other way? The prince kisses the frog? That doesn't sound right. Why doesn't it sound right? Why is there something about a woman kissing a frog that sounds "right" and a man kissing one that doesn't? Is there some gender thing at work here? Back to poison. Why are the frogs colorful? Wouldn't that attract predators to them? When I don't want to be noticed I don't wear hot pink.

Note that the student writing about frogs paused early in his freewrite, criticizing himself and maybe the assignment. He then noticed that he raised some interesting *questions*:

- Are toads and frogs different?
- Why do princesses kiss frogs in stories?
- What memories does he have about frogs?

As he stepped back again and read through this additional freewriting with a group of classmates, the student made use of his critical muscle and decided he liked *the question*, "Why do only princesses get to kiss the frog in fairy tales?" Here's how he drafted a mini-essay from there:

STUDENT EXAMPLE
"Frogs"

When it comes to frogs, one common occurrence in fairy tales is that the frog is seen as an ugly being, perhaps not taken seriously by most. However, at the same time, frogs in tales seem to have a habit of getting into conversations with princesses quite easily. Maybe it's their seeming ugliness that somehow makes them seem safe? Whether they're safe or not, princesses do seem to enjoy talking to them.

Furthermore, those princesses can also have the power to transform them with a kiss. Why is it that only princesses have that power? Could a **prince** kiss a frog and help him out? I've never seen that, and it doesn't seem possible, at least in the world of fairytales I've heard about. Why not? I'd like to research it further, because I think it could tell me something about what children's fairytales are teaching them about gender. Maybe the princess, by kissing the frog, proves that she is a generous and open person, and not scared of a being who is supposedly different and even ugly? Is her generosity the message of the story?

If it is, it relies on the idea that frogs are ugly and unappealing. That can be quite a misperception, since some of them are quite beautiful. What if we imagine a frog in a fairy tale as one of those beautiful blue ones? Or am I getting too carried away with all this? After all, I'm just talking about frogs!

Another direction: Not sure if he liked this direction, the student went back to his original freewrite and wrote a second mini-essay, one that considered *a different question*: "Why do some frogs have bright colors?"

I have seen plenty of ordinary frogs in person, perhaps on a rock by the side of the lake or jumping around in grass as rain approaches.

But how about the more unusual frogs, the one with the colors? I've seen those only in pictures. A quick Google image search reveals some great ones—a beautiful "blue poison dart frog," or an electric-green one with bright red eyes. There's even a YouTube video called, "The 7 Most Beautiful Frogs in the World." Your idea of beauty might not be the same as theirs, but to me these frogs certainly are beautiful. Their colors look like they're wearing works of art.

Why did their colors develop that way? Wouldn't the colors attract predators? Or does it have something to do with their reproductive experiences? I'm guessing they use their beautiful skin to flirt. Who **wouldn't** be attracted to a turquoise coat threaded through with twisty brown lines? I'd like to know more about how that all works.

Thus the student has written drafts of two promising mini-essays. As you can see, seemingly "throwaway" freewrites can help you develop intriguing thoughts in many different directions if you allow your critical muscle to work with them.

PART ❷: CONSTRUCT YOUR MINI-ESSAY

- When you're ready to stop, after at least six or seven minutes, *bring in your critical muscle to read over your freewrite.*
- Find *an idea or question* in what you've written that you find intriguing. Maybe you haven't written it yet, and it emerges as you reread your freewrite. If you feel stuck, share your writing with someone and ask for help finding an idea or question in your freewrite.
- *Write a draft of your mini-essay* based on that idea or question, following any tangents that occur to you as you develop your idea.
- Shape your draft into at least two coherent paragraphs that follow a line of thinking about your idea or question. If they seem too long or contain different ideas, experiment with dividing them into multiple paragraphs.
- Read your draft aloud, ideally to a classmate or friend, paying attention to whether your overall perspective is consistent. For example, in the first Frog example above, the student's perspective was on gender issues. In the second, the student wrote with an artistic/scientific perspective. What overall perspective do you have?
- If you like, ask your classmate what they like best in your draft, and what they might like to hear more about or see you do differently.
- Read through and tweak again until you feel satisfied that your mini-personal essay works well as a whole.

PART ONE

Writing a Personal Essay

1

Get to Know the Personal Essay as a Genre and Move towards Your Own

EXERCISE 1
Your Initial Thoughts on Being Personal in Writing

Write or talk about the following questions:

- How do you feel about the idea of writing a personal essay?
- What, if anything, do you think might be most scary, or exciting, about it for you?
- Do you have topic(s) in mind that you'd like to write about, or types of topics?
- Are you more likely to be honest when talking, or when writing?

Share your thoughts with one or two classmates.

Have you noticed that one person in conversation can make the story of an ordinary trip to the store sound quite interesting, while someone else can talk about an exciting adventure and bore people in the telling? Why *is* that? Different people would answer that question differently, but your answer(s)

will help guide you toward writing the kind of personal essay that you yourself find engaging and satisfying to write.

My goal in this section is for you to write a personal essay in a way that suits both you and your readers. This week, you'll explore the personal essay genre and begin finding topics that suit you. In Chapter 2 you will learn about potential personal essay structures as you begin drafting your essay. In Chapter 3 you will polish and revise your draft with feedback from others.

What Is a Personal Essay?

I define a personal essay quite loosely as one in which the reader learns something significant, and true, about who the writer is as a person. Its subject matter is open, ranging from autobiographical narratives to reflections on ideas.

One wonderful thing about personal essay writing is that your topic—*you*—has built-in interest to you as a writer. Let's face it, we usually find ourselves quite fascinating. Uncovering layers of your own thinking can be difficult at times, but it's always at least a little bit enjoyable. And when you enjoy the process of writing a personal essay, your reader will probably enjoy your work too.

By "enjoy" I don't necessarily mean having what you might normally think of as a "good time," though of course that could happen. Enjoyment as a personal essay writer and reader might mean deep engagement not only with pleasurable stories, but also with painful, confusing, or frustrating elements of your experience and thinking.

Writing a personal essay requires you to be honest not only with the reader but with yourself. You should also be artful, meaning that you shape and present your experience in a compelling way. Personal essays are sometimes seen as **creative nonfiction**, which means they incorporate strategies used by fiction writers and poets—scene-setting, characterization, dialogue, and voice—in service of rendering "true" experience. *Readers expect* that you will say something true and interesting about yourself, and that you will shape it into a form that is intriguing and imaginative.

Many students come to college or university having written a particular kind of admissions essay, aimed at expressing something of the student's personality and experience. There are excellent examples of this genre; maybe you wrote one yourself.

A "college essay" is both personal and an essay, though it is usually quite different from what I'd define as the genre of personal essay. The main goal of the college admissions essay is to support your application, which means that if you wrote one you needed to show yourself in your very best light. Even if you wrote about difficulties or hardships, you probably highlighted them in a way that demonstrated qualities that made you *look good*: grit, hard work, resilience, and whatever else you thought the admissions committee would value.

You could certainly demonstrate such qualities in a personal essay too, but your goal now is very different from wanting readers to accept you into an institution. It's to *engage them in depth in your actual lived thoughts and experiences*. Readers of personal essays are open to your honest acknowledgement of your flaws and doubts. Unlike college admissions committees, they don't mind at all if you express things about yourself that you are not necessarily proud of. In fact, they will most likely be curious to hear more about those.

You might be reluctant to acknowledge your flaws in an essay. Maybe you think it's just too, well, *personal* to do so. Or on the other hand you might worry that when you write about your flaws or doubts, they might sound like clichés, leading to the kinds of insights that other people have already written about. Those concerns make sense—let's look more closely at them for a moment.

Yes, personal essays are personal. The whole point of writing them is to write about your personal experience, and the whole point of reading them is to learn about a writer's personal experience. Most of us want to share at least *some* of our experiences and inner reflections with readers, even when that might mean exposing quirky ideas or faults.

Perhaps you are the kind of person who loves to talk about yourself. If so, you may be a natural for the personal essay genre. But even if you love talking about yourself, and especially if you don't, writing personal essays can make you feel shy.

"There's no way I'll put these thoughts on paper for everyone to see!" you might think, at some point in the process.

I get that. Being seen can be scary, especially if you didn't necessarily choose to do it. Maybe you didn't realize that your class would involve personal writing, or maybe you're in the class by mistake, and really do not want to express your personal thoughts at all.

Don't drop the class! When you write a personal essay, *you are in control of the material*. *You have plenty of choice* when it comes to topics, and you can find your own comfort zone between exposure and privacy. You certainly do *not* have to write about any topic you don't want to write about. And many "personal" topics don't reveal anything private or autobiographical— you can write a wonderful personal essay solely about how you *think* about something. For example, here's what a student wrote when looking at DVDs in the library. This is certainly personal-essay-style writing, though it doesn't tell us anything about the writer's life.

STUDENT EXAMPLE
A Student's Personal, but Not Autobiographical, Writing

It always makes me a little sad to see the wall in the library piled with DVDs. I know nobody will check these lonely DVDs out, so I don't know why they are still kept there. Maybe if my computer had a disk drive I could find one of them a loving home, if only temporarily. The DVDs are on their own unique form of death row, cast out from their other electronic peers and waiting until they will eventually be disposed of. I turn a blind eye on these helpless victims of creative destruction. Does my bystander behavior here make me no better than the streaming services that have evicted these DVDs from their homes? These DVDs are subjected to eternal torture, inches away from curious students who will never pick them up. But maybe they're fine with that. They had their moment; nobody is going to be young forever. They served multiple generations with entertainment ... Perhaps they prefer to be in this space, out in the open with other DVDs instead of filed away in solitary confinement under a dusty cabinet. I prefer to believe in this latter interpretation. It makes me feel more at ease and allows me to finally begin my homework. (GK)

The Problem of Clichés

People often criticize each other for saying things that are clichéd, meaning that other people have already said them, many times. You might wonder, as a personal essayist, whether the issues and questions you think about are those that others have pondered before you. And if so, how big a problem is it if you include such thoughts in a personal essay? Well, it depends.

We certainly don't have to think of brand-new subjects every time we write. If we did, there would be only a tiny number of successful writers in the world. Most personal essay subjects—love, pain, doubt, transformation, etc.—have been covered countless times by other writers. However, no matter what your essay's subject is, there is a way to write about it as only *you* can.

Let's say you're writing a personal essay about the time your team won the game. Your story might have much in common with experiences others have had—maybe some painful previous losses, hard work, a helpful (or difficult) coach, team drama, etc. Can you write your own essay about winning the game that's different even from one written by your teammate?

Yes, you can! But to avoid clichés, your job is to find the details that are *specific to your own experience.* Maybe your sister helped you practice at 5:00 a.m., or you had a blister you decided to ignore, or there was someone on the other team you felt intensely jealous of—the more you get into details, the more you'll write the essay only you can write about winning that game.

Sometimes your starting topic will shift as you explore it. For example, a student of mine recently decided that he wanted to write his personal essay about the question, "Why do bad things happen to good people?" It's certainly a legitimate question, but is there an answer? The student's initial plan for his essay was to describe three good people, and then explain how bad things happened to each one.

As he told me about that plan, I had to tell him that it seemed flat to me. "It's not news to anyone that bad things happen to good people, and since you have no clear answer to why they do, your essay would confirm something that everyone already knows, without taking it anywhere," I said.

That didn't deter him. "Okay," he responded. "So could I write on that topic in a different way somehow?" I advised him to do a freewrite about it: Why is the topic so important to you? What motivates you to think you want to write about it?

As he did the freewrite, the student realized that his motivation was the fact that he himself wanted to be good but had an inner voice telling him that it didn't matter, because bad things could easily happen to him no matter how he behaved. Aha! A promising wrinkle to his topic.

"Can you write about a specific way in which you've wanted to be good, exploring your inner experience at a particular moment in your life?" I asked. He could. In fact, he realized that he had gotten to the root of his original question and could tell the story of his specific experience and his reflections about it.

It makes sense to be somewhat wary of subjects and ideas that many writers have already explored in detail. But if, like that student, you are willing to trace back through your reasons for wanting to write about something, you can get yourself on the right track toward writing a personal essay that no one but you could write.

Finding Your Personal Essay Topic with a Journal of Noticings

How do you arrive at a viable topic? Maybe you already have one in mind, at least as a starting point. But if not, you know there *must* be many intriguing personal topics for you to write on. And yet when asked to pull just one, your mind might go blank.

Sometimes the problem is that your critical muscle is struggling to find the "perfect" topic. It discards possibilities because they don't seem alive or important enough to write about. Relax! Virtually any starting point from your life has the potential to take you in workable directions, even if you can't yet imagine what your final essay is about or what it might look like.

Don't settle on a topic simply because it seems easiest, or because someone told you it was a good topic. The key is to start with a memory, idea, or question *that you personally find compelling.*

"I don't know what to write," you might say, "but I wrote my college-entrance essay on how much I learned from my grandfather, so I'll just write about that again for my personal essay." Your grandfather might well be a subject you want to explore further, but please don't choose to rehash material you already wrote in the past because you think it's easier. Doing so would probably bore not only you, but your readers.

Of course, many writers return over and over to the same topic(s) because they want to explore them from different angles. In fact, most of us find that our writing circles around a particular set of themes we find fascinating. That's not a problem at all, as long as we don't simply keep writing *the same essay* we wrote in the past. That's unacceptable in a college class and can be punishable as academic dishonesty. But more importantly for our purposes, if your writing isn't alive and interesting for you as a writer, why bother?

"But I don't even have a starting point!" you might say. "There's nothing I have super strong feelings about right now. I can't think of anything!" I've heard those words often from students, and I've felt them myself too.

A **Journal of Noticings** can help solve that problem.

PUBLISHED EXAMPLE
Assembling Fragments of Everyday Life

What we call "inner life" is a permanent flashing in the brain that wants to take shape as voice, as writing ... for me [at age 17] ... writing had, essentially, eyes: the trembling of a yellow leaf, the shiny parts of the coffee maker, my mother's ring with the aquamarine that gave off a sky-blue light, my sisters fighting in the courtyard, the enormous ears of the bald man in the blue smock. I wanted to be a mirror. I assembled fragments according to a before and an after, I set one inside the other, a story came out. It happened naturally, and I did it constantly. (Ferrante 41–42)

What Do You Notice?

As freewriting teaches us, our minds are never actually blank. Even when we may think they are, a multitude of perceptions is flitting through our heads.

"That bird has an interesting way of looking at me," you might observe as you're walking along. If someone is with you, you might call their attention to it as a passing thought that soon disappears; if you're alone, the thought might dart in and out and be forgotten forever. That's what I'll call a *noticing*. We all have many noticings throughout the day. You might think everyone around you notices the same things you do, but they don't. Walking into a classroom before a class begins, say, one person might notice that three students are wearing the same style of sweatshirt. Another might see that one of the chairs has a wobbly leg. Another might be preoccupied by the worry that their pants don't look good on them. Another might notice a fellow student who looks depressed. Someone else might be mentally rehashing an idea they learned about in their previous class.

When *you* walk into a room, what are you more likely to notice?

- The furniture and décor
- People's clothes
- People's emotions
- Your own thoughts
- The interactions between people
- The music playing, or any other sounds
- How people perceive you
- Something else?

When you walk outside, what do you tend to notice most?

- Weather
- Landscape and vegetation
- Architecture
- People's moods
- People's ethnicities
- People's outfits
- Something else?

When you think about the world, what kinds of thoughts or concepts interest you most?

- Philosophical reflections
- The natural world
- How things are constructed
- News about friends or celebrities
- The arts—which one(s)?
- Social categories—gender, race, class, ethnicities
- Politics and activism
- Religion
- Psychological interactions and truths
- Something else?

MAIN ASSIGNMENT

Keep, and Write from, a Journal of Noticings, in Three Parts

PART ❶: COLLECT YOUR NOTICINGS

Personal essay writers, like artists of any sort, often seek out their random noticings and write them down in case they might be useful in an essay. Keeping a Journal of Noticings is a way to collect such thoughts. It can help you find a personal essay topic that really works for you, or explore new angles on a topic you already have.

- *Pay more attention to whatever you are struck by.* Don't force anything—just observe what you notice. Many of your noticings may be external—what you perceive with your senses. But internal noticings—memories, emotions, questions, struggles—are important for your list too.
- *If you have an idea in mind for your personal essay,* feel free to include thoughts that occur to you about it as part of your noticings.
- *Find a way that pleases you to collect* your noticings: in a notebook, or on a device or voice recorder.
- *You might bring your notebook with you to record your noticings as they come to you, or else take time each day to make your list* of what you remember noticing.
- *Keep your list for at least a few days,* not worrying about what it adds up to.

STUDENT EXAMPLE
Selections from a Student's Journal of Noticings: From Cafeteria to Biology

- I notice that girls in the cafeteria often head for salad and vegetables, whereas most guys usually go for meat
- I notice that music always changes my mood
- I notice that I get annoyed when a certain person whose name I won't mention talks, but I really am not sure why the person bothers me so much

- I notice that a certain friend of mine seems less happy than she used to be
- I notice that unlike some people, I like it when the weather is cold and rainy and we have to wear warmer clothes
- I notice that I like math class more than biology, and I thought it would be the other way around (JT)

STUDENT EXAMPLE

Selections from a Student's Journal of Noticings: "I Am Always Thinking"

- I've gotten better at saying no as I've gotten older. It's human nature to want to be liked, to be conflict averse in interactions with peers. However, in order to stay true to my own values and obtain the peace that I so deeply seek, I've learned how to say no when a potential decision doesn't align with my ethos in life.
- I've heard some people say that they feel pressure to live up to their last name. I think I understand what they mean when they say this, but I can't say that I've felt a similar pressure at all. That just isn't the dynamic in my family.
- I hear a lot of cries and pleas for justice (and rightfully so). I wonder to myself what it actually means for there to be justice, if it is a fixed constant, or something that changes over time. Certainly what people mean by justice in 2021 is different than those in the 1700s. It makes me wonder whether we can separate justice from our own idea of it.
- I feel that everyone wants to be the best. But part of one person being the best means that somebody is going to have to be the worst. Beyond that, many people are going to have to be in the middle, when they want to be the best. When I was younger I wanted to be the best in everything I did. Part of me still has this inclination, but I try now to only care about giving my best effort. If I give my best effort, I can live with whatever result comes from this.
- Unfortunately, I feel that I am always thinking. This is immensely helpful in school ... but in my personal life it can be challenging. Overthinking can lead to anguish if it is not managed properly. This is something I've made immense progress with, although it is a journey I am still undergoing. (GK)

PART ❷: CHOOSE A STARTING POINT

When you have a robust list, examine it, asking yourself some of the following questions:

- *What do I notice about my noticings?* Does my list tell me something about who I am and what kinds of things are in my mind?
- *Are there links between more than one noticing?* Can I put my noticings into categories? For example, categories could be along the lines of "observing others' feelings," "noticing colors and design," "tuning in to my own inner experiences," "thinking about science," "thinking about religion," "thinking about sports." What are my categories? Or maybe my noticings all seem random, and I don't see any links among them.
- *Which noticing(s) seem exciting to me* as a topic for more writing, even if I have no idea at all about what sort of essay might come of them? Which pull at me the most, for whatever reason?

PART ❸: WRITE FROM YOUR STARTING POINT

Choose one noticing, or category of noticings, as a starting topic for more writing. It should be an experience, question, or concept that you think has possibilities for exploration, even if you don't know exactly what those are. "I overthink too much," or "my family's move to the suburbs really messed me up," or whatever resonates from your list.

Once you have that starting-point topic, your next step is to begin a series of freewrites that will move toward the draft of your personal essay. We're still in the creative muscle stage of the process—it's not yet time to worry about the structure of your draft.

You might think that doing more unstructured writing once you have a topic is a waste of time. You want to get to the job of writing your actual essay right away! I get that, but I caution you not to fall into the trap of skipping the step of doing some exploratory freewrites from your topic first. Here's why: Let's say a student thinks, "one of my noticings is that it's a beautiful spring day. I'm going to write an essay about why I love spring! I'll structure it chronologically, by starting with a story about being a kid in the spring, then moving to describing how much I loved spring days in high school, and ending up with how I love spring just as much now."

Do you see why that might become a somewhat disappointing essay? An effective personal essay requires more texture or complexity, and freewrites can help the student dig deeper into why "beautiful spring days" are a rich topic for them.

By freewriting about "beautiful spring days," for example, they might discover that there isn't much pulsating for them in the topic, and that they should go back to their noticing and take time to find more. However, they also might realize that a "beautiful spring day" is the tip of a deep iceberg of experiences they want to explore.

As she was writing her novel *Mrs. Dalloway*, Virginia Woolf wrote regularly in her diary about her process. She described feeling that she was "tunneling" behind her characters, by which she meant that she sometimes interrupted the plot of the novel to explore what was going on in her characters' minds. "I dig out beautiful caves behind my characters," she said in her diary. "I think that gives exactly what I want; humanity, humour, depth ... it took me a year of groping to discover what I call my tunneling process, in which I tell the past by installments, as I have need of it" (*Writer's Diary* 66).

Freewriting from your starting point is a way of tunneling behind your own thoughts. You can't know in advance what tunnels could exist behind, or underneath, your chosen topic, but if something intrigues you as a topic, freewriting can lead you to the gems that are there to find. Try it!

With your starting-point topic in mind—I'll call it "T" for "topic"—begin on any prompt from the following list. Let your writing pull you somewhere, even if that means you abandon your original T for something new. *After about five minutes, keep going if you're on a roll, but if you're slowing down, pick another prompt and freewrite,* either continuing with T or a new version of T that has begun to emerge in your freewriting. Repeat with new prompts—at least three—for as long as you like, and make sure you generate at least two pages of raw writing.

- What is most interesting to you about T?
- What question(s) do you have about it?
- What person comes to mind when you think about T?
- What emotion, or mixed emotions, do you have about T?
- Does anything make you uncomfortable about writing or thinking about T?
- Can you write a dialogue that approaches a conversation you had, or can imagine having, about T?
- What would someone else you know, or know of, say about T?

- In the writing you've done so far, have you been leaving something out about T?
- Is there a specific story from your life that speaks to T for you? Write the story:
  - » What happened?
  - » How did you feel about it?
  - » Was anyone else involved in the story?
  - » Where did it take place?
  - » What time of year/time of day was it?
  - » Did you change your mind about anything that happened?

* * *

The freewriting that comes out of the above assignment most likely is "all over the place" and unstructured: the raw material for your personal essay. At some point you'll feel that you've had enough of the "messiness" of your explorations—that's a signal that your critical muscle needs to take over and start finding ways to put the pieces of your essay together in a way that makes sense to you and works for your reader. We'll work on that in the next chapter.

2

Find a Way to Structure and Compose Your Personal Essay

STUDENT EXAMPLE
Resisting "Cookie-Cutter" Structures

I love to write in short spurts. Small sentences with juicy adjectives and blunt images make my writing feel complete. I think everything I've written has tapped into different areas of my character. As a writer I am not afraid to speak the truth, to produce raw work that might feel uncomfortable to a distant reader ... The reader can learn from my writing how I love to write in a poetic fashion. I don't like cookie-cutter structures and I like to think outside the box. (OS)

Your freewrites can serve as building blocks that you re-arrange as you begin to shape your essay's structure. Here are some preliminary steps you can take with your critical muscle as you begin to shape your draft:

- *Read* through your freewrites, marking anything that strikes you as interesting.
- *Decide* which parts delight or intrigue you. Would they be interesting to write a whole essay about?
- *Share* your writings with someone else, but only if you want to. This isn't the time for criticisms of your draft; you're just looking for information about what a reader may find intriguing or want to know more about.
- *Choose* theme(s), scene(s), or question(s) that emerge for you.
- *Imagine* your audience: Personal essays allow you to speak in your own voice. But what *is* your voice, and who are you talking to in your personal essay? You have probably noticed that you speak differently depending on who is listening. A parent, a friend who loves you, a peer you don't know well, an authority figure, someone you dislike—even without doing it consciously, you rely on your instincts to shape your voice and tone to your audience. Having a specific "ideal reader" in mind—a specific person, or a stranger with genuine interest in you and your subject—can be useful.
- *Be open* to the story that "wants" to be told. It might seem odd to personify a story, as though it has a desire. And yet when I ask students, "What does this essay want to be about?" I'm rarely met with quizzical eyes. They usually understand what I'm getting at, even if they have never thought about it that way before. What does your inner knowing have to say about what your stories *want*?
- *Continue listening* to your inner knowing throughout the process of creating your essay. You might find yourself revising, deleting, and adding more of them as you go.
- *Read other personal essays* to get ideas about forms and structures.

Begin to Imagine Your Personal Essay's Structure

When you know what you want your essay to be about—maybe a narrative about a specific moment in your life, maybe a personal reflection, maybe your thoughts about something, or whatever else you've begun to explore in your freewrites—it's time to find a structure that will help you describe your experience and thoughts in a way that will get readers to appreciate them most fully.

In contrast to personal essays, traditional academic essays often grow out of structures that are built into assignments. For example, many essays you write in college will be structured in the classic "thesis-and-proof" format (see also Chapter 6). They begin with a statement of a point of view—a **thesis**—and go on to provide evidence for it.

The structures of personal essays, in contrast, tend to be much more variable. By **structure**, I mean the decisions you make about how to organize your material: What should come first? Where should you go from there? What sort of organizing principle will work? If you want to write a personal essay about your problematic relationship with your brother, for example, it wouldn't necessarily be best to begin with an academic-sounding statement like, "in this essay I will demonstrate that my brother had some problematic effects on my life." It might work much better, say, to begin with the story of a specific moment with your brother, followed by a series of thoughts and stories that demonstrate your experience. Thinking along those lines begins your vision of the "structure" of your essay.

Of course, that statement about your brother *could* potentially work to begin your essay. Your purpose after stating it could be to dig into why you use the word "problematic" to describe your brother's effects on you and to question yourself about using that word. Maybe by the end of the essay we'd see your opening statement differently from the way it seemed at the start. You might have led us to a new understanding of "my brother had a problematic effect on my life," by structuring your essay around questions you ask yourself about your own assumptions.

One of the pleasures of writing personal essays, then, is also a difficulty—you have the freedom to create your own structures, but they also must leave the reader satisfied that you have presented your story in an intriguing and organized way. There are myriad ways to discover a structure that works for your essay's purposes. I say "discover," because an essay's structure often *grows out of* what you want to say, as opposed to being something you decide on before you write. Be flexible: if you try to set up a fixed structure for your essay before you've written anything, you might find that it doesn't hold up once you start writing.

Two Metaphors for Holding Essays Together

You might hear people use metaphors like **thread** and **scaffolding** to describe the through-lines that make well-crafted essays. I imagine a beautiful gold thread woven through an essay's bright red cloth, or I imagine an essay as a building, with stable wooden beams holding it up.

Both metaphors get at the idea that even if it's not explicitly stated, your essay needs to be built in a coherent way, with something solid holding it together. That something could be a kind of argument—"my brother messed me up"—but it could also be a question—"How can I best understand my brother?"—or another kind of exploration—"How has anger worked in my life?" or "What effect did that year my family spent in Portugal have on my brother and me as children?" All these could serve as *one-sentence organizing threads* or *scaffolds*, which help essays "hold up" or "hold together."

How does a personal essay writer best acquire such a thread, or, if you prefer, a scaffolding to hold it up?

Let's say the subject of my personal essay is "my father's experience as an immigrant from Greece, and what it was like for me as his American daughter." That's not a *thread* yet; it's a *subject*. For a thread, I have to *do* something with my subject. I might decide on something like, "while I deeply respect my father, I sometimes scoffed at his Greek ideas and habits when I was a child, and I want to explore my guilt and other feelings about that."

That thread would not necessarily be something I'd state explicitly in the essay itself. But it would be the idea I was "working" through the whole essay, and it would give me a framework for my draft. Here's how:

- I would use it to help me choose the specific stories I wanted to bring to life.
- I would ask myself questions about it, digging deeper into the reasons for the way I felt.
- I would always be able to return to it if I got stuck.
- I would discard potential stories that veered too far away from it.
- I would make sure that the essay addressed it all the way through, ending up with a perspective at the end that came to some closure about it.

To make my thread work at its best, I need to find a structure for my essay that I can weave it into.

Structures Used by Three Published Writers

The best way to get ideas for structuring your own essays is to examine structures created by a range of other writers. I don't present the following as structures to imitate (though you might experiment with that if you like), but in order to open your mind to possibilities.

Here are structures invented by three published writers:

- *Michele Morano's essay*, "In the Subjunctive Mood," is about a series of experiences she had while studying abroad in Spain, focusing on the somewhat undefined and changing feelings she had about her boyfriend. She structures the essay by *dividing it into sections, each headed by one of the rules in a Spanish-language textbook about when one might use the subjunctive mood.* In each section, she describes a particular moment from her life; the fact that the subjunctive is about doubt or uncertainty gives her a useful structure within which to reflect on her own evolving uncertainties.

- *Meghan Daum's essay*, "Music Is My Bag," plays with the idea of a tote bag with the title's slogan on it. She sarcastically defines "'music is my bag' culture" to describe an attitude about music that she sees, and resists, in other musicians. She structures her essay by *beginning with scenes involving people who carry tote bags with the slogan on them, moving to a discussion of her family's "music is my bag" culture, and then broadening out to "movies are my bag" and "sports are my bag" people,* all in service of exploring her own frustration with a certain cultural mindset.

- *Leslie Jamison's essay*, "The Empathy Exams" is a reflection on the complicated nature of empathy. She *divides her essay into sections, beginning with character studies of invented patients she was hired to impersonate in order to help doctors-in-training develop empathy. From there, she goes on to sections about her own experiences as a patient herself, interacting with her boyfriend's, and her doctors', different styles of empathy.* Those styles bothered her at first, but in reflecting on different types of empathy throughout the essay, she develops the idea of how her thinking has evolved when it comes to her understanding of empathy's possibilities.

None of these writers used fixed structures given to them by someone else. I imagine that they also didn't lay those structures out in advance of beginning to write their essays. Each structure seems to have evolved out of the writer's ongoing reflections about her topic.

The Five-Paragraph-Essay Structure and How One Student Moved Beyond It

You might know that when teachers talk about "the five-paragraph essay" we are not referring to *any* essay that has five paragraphs. We are describing a certain kind of fixed essay-structure that is taught to many students. Its five paragraphs are as follows:

- An introductory paragraph that expresses an idea or argument
- Three "body" paragraphs, each giving examples of that idea or support for the argument
- A concluding paragraph summing things up

Be wary of that structure—it is unlikely to contain a useful thread or scaffolding for an effective personal essay!

To demonstrate what I mean, I want to tell you the story of a first-semester student of mine—I'll call him Shay. When he came to my office to discuss the first draft of his first personal essay, Shay began our conversation by telling me that his goal in writing the essay was "to show the reader what a great time my family had on vacation in Mexico." He was proud to add that he had a clear five-paragraph structure in mind, the kind he had learned in high school, and that he believed it was working well. Here is how he described his essay's structure:

- *Paragraph 1*: Explain that I had a great time on my family trip to Mexico for three reasons: one, the weather was great; two, my family was in a good mood; and three, we did a lot of fun things.
- *Paragraphs 2, 3, and 4*: Each expands one of those reasons.
- *Paragraph 5*: Conclusion: it was a perfect vacation.

Would you want to read that essay? Maybe, depending on whether you cared about Shay the person, and what kind of narrator he was. His essay might also work well on a travel website, since if you were planning to go to the place you might be interested in the specifics of what he enjoyed.

But in the genre of personal essay, Shay's was not very interesting. It needed more.

I asked Shay how he felt about his draft.

"I like it!" he said. "It reminds me of how much fun my family had."

I was reluctant to disappoint him, but I had to. "I don't know," I said. "It's great that your family had fun, but I think readers need more. For example, I might want to know more about your family in particular—how are they different from everybody else who went to the same place in Mexico? Can you make your lived experience come alive for the reader more than you have so far?"

Shay was not happy with my comment at first. He enjoyed reliving his fun experiences through his own writing, and he figured that readers would too. However, he had to admit that he was also intrigued by the idea that the form he had learned so well in high school might not be the only way to structure his essay. He agreed to begin digging into the five-paragraph-essay structure to find out how to make use of the hidden gems that lurked within it.

I told Shay that as a responder to his essay I didn't want to pry into family stories that he might not want to tell. But I had to say that as a reader I was struck by his point: "my family was in a good mood."

"Would you maybe want to explore more about the idea of your family's mood?" I asked. At first, Shay hesitated.

"What do you mean?"

"Well, was your family *not* in a good mood when you *weren't* on vacation?"

"My Dad works long hours and is tired a lot. When we were in Mexico, he slept in. And when he woke up, the good side of his personality really came out."

"What was that like?"

"He was funny. He wanted to explore places."

"How about if you freewrite right now about your dad?" I asked. "Think of specific moments, not generalities. For example, as a reader I'd be curious to hear about a time when your father is not in a good mood and maybe a specific moment from your vacation that contrasts with that?"

Shay got the look on his face that writers get when they're beginning to think of ideas. He found a corner right outside my office and did a freewrite for about ten minutes. When he came back, he told me that his freewrite began to evolve into a reflection about who his father really is, in contrast to who he so often seemed to be when drowning in work. His freewriting led him to the idea of exploring how he himself had qualities in common with his dad, like becoming irritable when busy to the point that he was somewhat rude to his friends. Why *was* that? He did not know the answer and wanted to explore further. It turned out that Shay's initial idea for a five-paragraph essay about his family's vacation was just the tip of the iceberg of some thinking that he wanted to do about his family, especially his father.

By the time Shay got to his final version of the essay, he had a very different structure from that of his five-paragraph essay draft. The thread holding his essay together had become Shay's series of insights:

- His observation of his father at home—irritable and overworked
- His pleasure when he saw his father joyful in a specific moment on the beach in Mexico
- His perception that his father's moods were dependent on external circumstances
- His realization, one night on the beach looking at the moon, that he too had such moods
- His conversation with his father about the similarities between the two of them in terms of moods
- His conclusion that he wanted to be different from his father in some ways and to encourage his father to be different, too

These six elements were not each in separate paragraphs—each of them spanned a few shorter paragraphs that included dialogue and description. Shay was impressed at how much he had to say, and he ended up writing a far longer and more interesting essay than he had expected.

I tell this story to illustrate two things: first, how the five-paragraph essay in itself can often be unsatisfying and shallow even to its writer, and second, that if you do write such an essay but allow it to be a draft that you will revise, it could end up becoming an excellent springboard to more interesting writing. The key is not to stop too soon. The seeds of where Shay wanted to go were there in his first draft; he just needed time and work to develop them.

That is not to say that everyone should begin their personal essays by constructing a five-paragraph structure as a springboard. Not at all. In fact, Shay may have gotten to his idea about his father more quickly if he had begun differently. My point here is simply that he got to the essay only he could write by (1) getting out his first thoughts, and then (2) digging into what was underlying those first thoughts to find a structure that worked for him.

Five Templates for Structuring Your Personal Essay and Their Challenges

The following are some general templates for personal essays that might help you conceive of your draft's overall structure. Feel free to use one of them to structure your draft if you think it serves your purpose.

Template 1: Chronological Order

Tell the story in the order in which it happened.

CHALLENGES:

- *Where to begin.* How far back should you go to get to the "beginning" of the story? How much background will the reader need?
- *How can you build up to the point of your story?* What idea or question is your narrative exploring, and how can you "plant seeds" throughout the essay to develop it?
- *How much should you say about each moment in time?* Is it important to describe the dishes that were in the sink during an argument you had? Or that your friend Miguel was visiting?
- *How to conclude?* Should you just stop when the story ends? Is there a concluding idea that you want to lead up to? How much should you say, if anything, about how you interpret the story?

Template 2: Before and After

Compare past and present experiences: I used to be (or feel or believe) X, but now I am/feel/believe Y.

CHALLENGES:

- *Deciding how, and when, to describe the "before."* What were you like? What did you used to think? Or what was the situation like?

- *Pinpointing the cause of the change.* Was it a moment of revelation? Did it evolve slowly, and if so, what made the changes? Your reader will want at least some discussion of why there's a difference between "before" and "after." If you aren't sure, you might say something along the lines of, "I am not sure why I am so different now. It could be A, it could be B, or maybe it's some kind of combination ..."
- *Establishing how things are different now.* The challenge is to do so in a way that makes the **difference** clear between "before" and "after."

Template 3: Frame

Use two narratives, one framing the other. For example, describe the present moment of walking through a house—that's the frame—interrupted by sections that flash back to past experiences with objects in that house. Or alternate one person's story—the frame—with someone else's, etc.

CHALLENGES:

- *Finding an effective frame.* Both stories should be compelling to you, and you should make satisfying connections between them.
- *Organizing examples to work as a coherent whole.* For example, if your present-time frame is walking through a house remembering the past, a reader might become impatient if your alternating stories all say the same thing: "here's one thing I remember," "here's another thing," "here's a third." How can the memories in different rooms each represent different responses, or build toward an idea? "I believed in Santa when I slept in the upstairs bedroom, but things were different when I moved downstairs, because ..."
- *Signaling to the reader that you are shifting from one story to the other.* You might signal shifts with spaces between sections, or headings, or perhaps the changing presence of a particular object (the chair that was once new but in a later section is now worn, say) or person. Or maybe the frame takes place at a different time of day, or a different season of the year, etc.

Template 4: Organizing Concept or Object

Your essay could explore a single concept from various angles. The concept can be an emotion—empathy, sadness, joy, disappointment, etc.; it could be a concept—sacredness, cosmopolitanism, Generation Z. You could also use something concrete—say a coffee mug, or a building, to serve as your essay's central point.

CHALLENGES:

- *Being open to quirky overall themes.* Philip Lopate wrote "My Drawer," in which he lists the contents of one of his drawers, and in doing so manages to tell us quite a bit about who he is: "... this morning I have an urge to make an inventory of the drawer, in a last attempt to understand the symbolic underpinnings of my character" (91–94).
- *Finding a compelling concept/object.* It should be something that touches you in some way and has a complex meaning for you.
- *Creating a satisfying whole.* You need some kind of strategy for ordering your ideas. For example, Zadie Smith's strategy in her essay "Joy" is the idea that "joy" and "pleasure" are very different. We have to read more to understand her personal idea about the difference. She begins by briefly, and vaguely, mentioning the six times in her life in which she felt actual joy, and in the course of the essay, she indirectly describes each of those times, but not in a systematic way—we have to read closely to keep track of them. By the end we understand her point about how those "joy" experiences gave her something very different from "pleasure."

PUBLISHED EXAMPLE
From "Joy," by Zadie Smith

A lot of people seem to feel that joy is only the most intense version of pleasure, arrived at by the same road—you simply have to go a little further down the track. That has not been my experience. And if you asked me if I wanted more joyful experiences in my life, I wouldn't be at all sure I did, exactly because it proves such a difficult emotion to manage....

... I experience at least a little pleasure every day ... Until quite recently I had known joy only five times in my life, perhaps six, and each time tried to forget it soon after it happened, out of the fear that the memory of it would dement and destroy everything else ... Let's call it six. Three of those times I was in love ... twice I was on drugs ... Once

> in water, once on a train, once sitting on a high wall, once on a high hill, once in a nightclub, and once in a hospital bed ... (145–51)

Template 5: Question and Answer

You can structure your essay by posing a question and exploring various answers in the course of your essay.

CHALLENGES:

- *Finding an effective question.* An effective question is preferably one you don't have a simple answer to. It could be along personal lines, as in, "Why did I stop playing the piano when my father wanted me to continue?" It could also be theoretical—"Why would a person major in philosophy?" or "What is the role of anger in Buddhism?"
- *Choosing an effective order of ideas.* Once you have the question, you have to figure out how to introduce it—should you start with the question, or give some background first? From there, will you organize your essay as a narrative, or would it work better as a collection of separate sections? If so, what order should those be in, and what will hold them together?

Work with Your Chosen Structure

No first draft is a great personal essay—they *always* must evolve.

In deciding on a structure for your essay, pay attention to the specific story, idea, or question *that nudges at you from within your ideas.* Have you had the experience of starting to write about one idea and then finding that another one is pulling you in a different direction? It's a somewhat mysterious process, but that nudge can help you find the potential direction, and structure, of your essay.

You might have a structure you think you like, except that it seems to slip away from you as your draft proceeds. That might mean finding more ways to make it work; it might also mean that you need another structure that is better suited to your purpose. Allow yourself time to make changes.

Here are some questions to consider as you work with your freewrites to construct your draft:

- *What's your favorite part of your idea so far?* It can often work best to focus in on that idea first. Write it out fully, and after that you can figure out what the rest of the essay should look like.
- *Do you have a potential thread in mind yet?* If the answer is no, keep writing—trust that you'll find one later. Once you do, write it down in a place where you can refer to it often. It could be vague, along the lines of, "I want to use tote bags with 'music is my bag' printed on them to make a point about the kind of people my parents were." Your preliminary thread will orient you as you work on your essay, but don't let it box you in. *Be open to letting it evolve* as you continue writing. Remember that Shay's original plan was, "I want to talk about what a great vacation my family had," and eventually evolved into "exploring what I learned about my father's moods and how they compare to mine."
- *What should the opening of your essay be?* Maybe—or maybe not—it's the chronological beginning of your story. Do you need background before you get to that? Or might it work better to start with a specific scene in the middle of your story, followed by a flashback? There are many possibilities.
- *Which people will you describe in detail?* Instead of "we were walking down the street," it's often effective to name participants: "my friend Jamar and I were walking...." The name alone might be enough; you can also decide whether the reader needs background on Jamar, or anyone else.
- *Which moments from the story are worth narrating in detail?* Any story you tell, even if it's about your thinking, is made up of various moments. Is "we went to the store" enough for your purposes, or are the details of the journey—"his red car was making weird noises as we drove to the store"—relevant to your goal in the essay? Is "I was annoyed" enough, or is "I had just heard that I got a C on the essay I had worked on for two weeks" important to the story?
- *As you write*, pause to do more freewriting when you find an idea you need to flesh out.
- *Stop periodically to rethink your thread. Has it changed?* It might continue to evolve as you write more.

While writing, you might be struck by a new organizing thought. For example, I imagine that Michele Morano probably realized in a sudden flash that she could organize her essay about her experience in Spain by starting each section with a rule from a Spanish language textbook. Another writer might decide to tell his story from his sister's perspective; another to use the couch in their living room as an organizing focus. Ideas that could work for your essay may grow out of your experience of writing, even if they weren't in your mind at all as you began your draft—be open to them!

When You're Ready, an Outline Can Be an Effective Map for Your Draft

It can be stifling to write an outline before you've written anything, but once you have pieces of writing to work with an outline can be very valuable, because it allows you to stand back from your work and envision an overall structure.

You don't need Roman numerals in straight columns (though use them if you like!). By "outline," I mean a clear idea of what goes where. Here's an example: "begin with the question about jealousy, go into that time in high school, move to my conversation with Carla, and then explain how I answer the question now." Such a list might not mean much to anyone but you, but it can be the start of an outline of the backbone of your essay.

STUDENT EXAMPLE
Rough Outline of an Essay with a "Before and After" Structure

ONE: Last year: Dialogue with John
- He asked if I felt jealous, because he did
- My answer of "no" and why it surprised him

TWO: Two years ago with Trish, maybe also as dialogue
- Scene in the auditorium—I was angry at her for her flirty role in the play
- She asked what was wrong
- I didn't say anything because I thought I was just angry for no reason

THREE: Last week, conversation with Carla
- Me saying some things shouldn't be said aloud
- Her view of being honest with herself about negative emotions

- Me reflecting back to Trish and how my anger pushed me away from her. What if I had been honest with myself and her?

FOUR: Present time
- Rethinking my thoughts about jealousy and feelings
- Plans for dealing differently with Carla
- Thinking of conversation with John and my answer now would be "yes"

MAIN ASSIGNMENT

Draft Your Personal Essay

Topic: Use any personal story or thought process that has arisen from your previous freewrites on your topic (T). It will continue to evolve as you work on your draft.

Structure: Keeping in mind what we learned about various potential structures and how other writers worked with them, shape a structure for your essay that suits your topic and your audience. Don't hesitate to make use of a structure, like "before and after," from our examples. You can make it your own!

Feedback: At some point in the process of drafting your essay, share it with others, perhaps in a peer feedback group (see Part Five).

Get Feedback on Your Draft and Revise It

EXERCISE 1
Share Your Draft with Peers and/or Your Teacher

Before they read it, share your process with them:

- How do you think your draft is going?
- What do you think it needs?
- What questions do you have for your readers?
- What is your favorite part about it so far?

As you read your peers' drafts (see feedback guides in Part Five) privately note what you learn from them about what you might want to do or not do in your own essay.

In this chapter, we'll look at some additional considerations and strategies that might help you add texture to your draft as you revise.

Plant a Seed of the Thread

This mixed metaphor helps me describe an important move at the beginning of a personal essay.

By "seed," I mean an idea, image, object, etc., that appears early in your essay to point the reader in a certain direction that you follow up on later as you develop your "thread." You don't have to decide on a seed at the start of drafting your essay, but it's useful to be open to possibilities as you draft; they may help you revise your introduction after the rest of the essay is done.

For example, imagine that you're writing about your experience studying abroad in France, and you've decided to use a "before-and-after" structure in which your thread is the story of your changed perception of what it means to learn a language. Maybe your introductory paragraphs tell the story of your impatience a few years ago with a student in your high school from Ecuador, Julio, who struggled with English. One day he asked you, "Put this *in* the table or *on* the table?"

"Come *on,*" you thought, annoyed. "It's not very complicated; why can't you get it right?"

That anecdote could be the seed for your own story of struggling with prepositions while abroad. Your essay could begin with it, and then move toward that day in France when you weren't sure whether to use *à* or *de* and suddenly had a memory of Julio, with new understanding of how the use of "in" and "on" could seem quite arbitrary to an English learner. Describing your sudden guilt about not having understood Julio back then could be a satisfying piece of your essay's scaffolding.

The seed's significance does not have to be clear to the reader at first. It can work like a glimpse of a seemingly random person in a movie's opening shot, who eventually turns out to be the movie's most important character. The reader will be satisfied to find out only later why you mentioned something seemingly random at first.

A seed could also simply set a mood. Let's say your essay is about your aunt's death, and your first section is a happy, remembered scene of doing something fun with her. The seed could be your pause for a moment to say you saw an autumn leaf, even though it was summer. Yes, that's a bit of a cliché, so maybe instead you'd choose something else—the time your aunt said, "I never want to be old," or ...?

Add Dialogue

Think about the difference between, "I snuck out of the house that night and we had a good conversation," and something like:

> "I'm out here," he whispered. The window screen stuck for a moment, but I lifted it, put one leg out, and slipped out of my first-floor bedroom. I took his hand and we ran across the grass, beyond the lights of the house.
>
> "I can't believe you did that!" he said as we started walking more slowly. Like me, he was excited and happy. His hand was so warm.
>
> "I have some things to tell you," I said.

> (Note that each time there is a new speaker, the convention is to put their comments, in quotations, in a new paragraph.)

Dialogue enhances personal writing, bringing readers right into the moment. You might want to include sections of dialogue in your essay.

However, you might hesitate to do so since you don't remember the exact words anyone used, and your essay is supposed to describe what *really happened*.

Personal essay writers have a concept of "emotional truth" to describe our orientation toward dialogue in non-fiction essays. We might not remember the exact words, but when we can describe an experience in a way that feels emotionally true to what actually happened, it can work well. You don't remember the exact words, but you do remember the scene, and the effect the words had, so you can write dialogue that is as close as possible to what you actually remember.

EXERCISE 2
Experiment with Dialogue in Your Draft

Find a moment from your draft in progress where a conversation occurred and write out the dialogue in a way that feels emotionally true to you. Might it enhance your essay?

Introduce Yourself to the Reader

In "On the Necessity of Turning Oneself into a Character," essayist Phillip Lopate points out that, unless you're famous, when you write a personal essay you have to keep in mind that your reader doesn't know anything about who you are beyond what you tell them. Since you can't define every aspect of yourself in a single essay, you have to make decisions about what details to reveal to the reader, just as a fiction writer would choose pertinent facts about a character.

Keep in mind that saying "I" means something very specific to you, but it means nothing to the reader without your explanations. Is it significant to your essay that you're writing as a student, as a person of your nationality, as a person of your gender, age, ethnicity, or sexual orientation? That's up to you to decide; what you tell the reader in a personal essay should form a "character" that represents a relevant piece of who you are.

You can be more honest in a personal essay than you might be in other forms. For example, you can tell your reader what you're actually thinking as you write, including your doubts. Imagine that you're writing an essay about your friend Miko, with the goal of explaining how upset you were about the fact that she got to be friends with your best friend and excluded you. Halfway through describing her, you might suddenly feel that you're not giving the reader a fair idea of what Miko is like.

You could then stop and say, "But wait. In the portrait I'm painting of Miko she sounds like an unpleasant person. That might be true to a degree, but I don't think you'd feel that way about her when you first met her. In fact, she's a very interesting person—let me give you an example ..."

You might even go more "meta," with a statement like, "I'm worrying as I write this because I'm not giving you a good idea of what Miko is really like. Why am I doing that? Am I trying to get you on my side unfairly? Do I want you to dislike Miko? That's terrible of me! So I'll tell you another true story about her that maybe will give you a better idea of her, and, maybe it will also give you a better idea of me, because ..."

In other words, whatever you're actually feeling or thinking while you write can make its way into your personal essay if you want to share it. That kind of self-revelation is part of what can make personal essays so interesting.

Keep in mind that when you tell a story from your life your reader knows nothing about your inner experience beyond what you choose to tell them. That could mean saying something like, "I was angry because three months earlier, he ..." or it could also be less direct—"after he said that, my hands got into fists in my pocket and I clenched them, hard."

Here are some ways you might put your inner experience onto the page:

- *Directly*: "I felt sad ..."
- *Indirectly*: "I ran in the other room as tears gathered in my eyes."
- *With direct quotations*: "I walked into the room. 'Wow, these people look guilty,' I thought."
- *Signaling with a different kind of font*: For example, italics: "I walked into the room. *These people look guilty.* I sat in the corner."
- *With a separate section(s)*: Tell just the facts of the story in Part One of your essay, and use Part Two to get into your feelings.
- *With a back-and-forth structure*: You could alternate sections between those describing facts and those describing feelings.
- *With headings for various parts of your essay*: For example, "(1) the story; (2) my inner truth; (3) rethinking." Use your imagination to make the headings your own.

The challenge with the above ideas is to *be consistent* with them. You train the reader when you use italics to indicate emotions, for example, and if you use italics elsewhere in the essay for a different reason, or if you indicate emotion without italics, your reader will be unnecessarily confused.

Details Are Crucial

Students sometimes tell me they think specific details don't matter in their essays, because it's fine for the reader to imagine details based on their own experience. This perspective sometimes comes up in peer feedback groups.

One day, I was sitting at my desk in class while students were working on their own in peer groups. I eavesdropped on one group's conversation.

"I like the fact," a peer responder said, "that you don't give us the details—I'm not sure exactly what you're getting at in that experience you had lying by yourself on that field, but that's fine—it lets me imagine how I might have felt if I had been in the same place."

"Really?" I thought. "I couldn't disagree more." I happen to have read that student's draft, and I knew she described sitting outside on our college's quad. Losing herself in contemplation of a blade of grass, she entered a kind of dream world filled with images and voices. I couldn't tell from her writing whether she had drifted into a memory, was having some kind of out-of-body experience, or was under the influence of something. I wanted to know! But in her peer group, she was nodding her head in agreement with the responder who *liked* her vague language.

I usually avoid intervening in student group work, but I had to speak up.

"Sorry to invade your group, but I have to disagree," I said. "I think your essay will be much more interesting if we get a clearer understanding of your experience. Yes, we might enjoy imagining our own experiences lying on grass, but we'll probably do that no matter what you say. The more we learn the specifics of what was happening to *you*, the more likely we'll be to read on.

"In fact," I went on, "if my experience of reading your essay is that I feel trapped in vague language, I'm less likely to think of my own experiences than I am to stop reading because the essay isn't 'giving' me enough."

The student was a good sport about that criticism, especially when her peers reluctantly agreed that I might be right. When she finally explained that the blade of grass transported her to her experience a few years ago when she was camping out in her home country of Brazil, her peers had to admit that they were much more intrigued, and they encouraged her to say more.

Bringing a Place to Life

Just as readers require that you show them who you are as a narrator, they rely on you to help them see the places you describe.

For example, if you write, "I walked out of the house," a reader might imagine a red colonial on a tree-lined street, or a unit in an apartment complex opening onto a long hall. To bring them into what *you* picture, be more specific: "I walked out of the tiny yellow cottage, noticing that the group of daffodils next to the crumbling front stoop were just about to bloom."

In bringing a place to life there are endless details to choose from, and it's up to you to select the ones that are important to the story your essay wants to tell. Will it make a difference if the reader knows what town or country a place is in? If it's morning, or late at night, or winter?

If you're not sure what to say, consulting your five senses can be useful:

- *Sight.* What does the place look like? Are there people around? Who are they? Is it indoors or outdoors? If indoors, what are some details of the furnishings? What's on the walls? How big is the room/rooms?

If outdoors, what is the setting of the streetscape or landscape? What vegetation is visible, if any?

- *Sound.* What do you hear in the place, including explicit sounds like music or people talking, or birds, wind, traffic, the refrigerator, etc. Is the place noisy or quiet? Are the sounds relevant or incidental to the scene you describe?

- *Smell.* Are there explicit smells, like those from food cooking, flowers, candles, or the steakhouse nearby? Is there a mixture of competing smells?

- *Touch.* Are the people in your essay sitting, standing, or moving? What do their chairs feel like, or the ground/earth beneath their feet? Does someone touch you or anyone else? Do you brush against a tree or a door? How do your clothes feel?

- *Taste.* What does any food in your story taste like? Is there a metaphorical taste of anything in the air?

An Aside: Human Geography

There's increasing attention in the academic world to how the place where something happens is an important factor in what happens there. The field of "human geography" has relevance across the curriculum, with scholars exploring everything from how air, water, and soil quality affect residents of a place to the relationship between our psychology and the landscapes we live in. You can join in such discussions as a personal essayist, either by researching elements of the place you're writing about or simply by reflecting on your own and others' experiences there.

Novelist and essayist Will Self begins his collection of personal writings about place, *Psychogeography*, by defining the study in his title in two ways. First, he says, psychogeography involves someone looking at place and being "... concerned with the personality of place itself" (11), independent of any one person's perspective. Try it: consider the place you're in right now. Could you describe its personality? What are its important moods, or features?

Self's second characteristic of psychogeography brings in the "personal" and consists of "... minutely detailed, multi-leveled examinations of select locales that impact upon the writer's own microscopic inner-eye" (11). Everyone's inner eye registers different things, and writing a personal essay can be a fascinating way to reflect on how the places you describe affect your own "inner-eye." What do you see in your current place that others might not notice?

Such musing could lead you to bring in other elements of place that could be useful to explore, or at least mention, in your essay:

- *Weather*. What was it like? Did it change or evolve?
- *Season*. You could describe this directly, "spring was well underway by then," or indirectly, "it felt so good not to have to wear a jacket anymore; I felt the sun's warmth on my skin."
- *Time of day*. Is the fact that your story took place at 3:00 a.m., or noon, or 9:00 p.m. a significant factor? How is the place different at different times?
- *The general "vibe" that you perceive in the place*. Is it a happy street? A depressed one? How do you feel when you walk there, especially when you open yourself to impressions beyond your current, personal mood? Do other people feel differently?
- *The place's "personality."* How would people who live there describe it? How about visitors?

PUBLISHED EXAMPLE
From "Street Haunting," by Virginia Woolf (1927)

How beautiful a London street is then, with its islands of light, and its long groves of darkness, and on one side of it perhaps some tree-sprinkled, grass-grown space where night is folding herself to sleep naturally and, as one passes the iron railing, one hears those little cracklings and stirrings of leaf and twig which seem to suppose the silence of fields all round them, an owl hooting, and far away the rattle of a train in the valley. But this is London, we are reminded; high among the bare trees are hung oblong frames of reddish yellow light—windows; there are points of brilliance burning steadily like low stars—lamps; this empty ground, which holds the country in it and its peace, is only a London square, set about by offices and houses where at this hour fierce lights burn over ... desks where clerks sit turning with wetted forefinger the files of endless correspondences; or more suffusedly the firelight wavers and the lamplight falls upon the privacy of some drawing-room, its easy chairs, its papers, its china, its inlaid table, and the figure of a woman, accurately measuring out the precise number of spoons of tea ... (257–58)

STUDENT EXAMPLE
Relaxation Lake

The Great Sacandaga Lake located in the Adirondacks of upstate New York perfectly fits my definition of relaxation. What used to be a town inhabited by homes and businesses was intentionally flooded many decades ago to create what I know as "the lake." The lake runs about 30 miles long and a few miles wide. Surrounding the perimeter lie hundreds of motorboats, kayaks, canoes, and docks during the summer. Despite being a beautiful scene on the water, there's no big commercial businesses nearby, no cute touristy spots, or even cell phone service. It's the closest I've come to "the middle of nowhere." It's the darkest darkness I've ever experienced at night. It's the most peaceful place I know.

After years of failed fishing attempts, my favorite activity is to park a rustic lounge chair that probably has spiders crawling underneath it on the uneven rocks near the water. It would take a few tries to get positioned comfortably and on stable footing, but once situated, I'd feel the best I ever do. Thankfully my phone isn't lighting up with notifications or is even useable, so I have no excuse but to appreciate the scenery. There is a little cove with a couple of properties to the left, and the same to the right. An older couple is likely putting along on a modest motorboat, and a kid flying on a tube off in the distance. The topography of the distant mountains is imprinted in my mind, as well as the constellations at night. Unlike the city, there are no funky smells or unpleasant sights. Only the occasional bug could possibly disturb a guest of the lake. (TG)

Dealing with Emotions "Appropriately"

Emotions are inevitable when you're writing a personal essay. They might be prompted by your subject matter; they might also arise out of the complexities of writing and revising. You might find those emotions difficult, exciting, scary, unbearable, or full of energy and promise.

When it comes to subject matter, some personal essay writers worry that bringing their emotions into an essay can be "inappropriate." Their impulse is to smooth such emotions over, so the reader barely notices them. That could be an effective strategy in some essays, in which, say, your goal is to tell a painful story without emotion so the reader feels the pain on their own. But at times, worrying about being "appropriate" puts a stranglehold on our creative muscle, preventing it from saying what we really need to say.

In her book about women's anger, Soraya Chemaly says, "If there is a word that should be retired from use in the service of women's expression, health, well-being, and equality, it is 'appropriate'—a sloppy, mushy word that purports to convey some important moral essence but in reality is just a policing term used to regulate our language, appearance, and demands. It's a control word" (261). This goes for people of any gender when it comes to writing, and too often we police ourselves out of fear of what readers will think of us.

Don't get me wrong—it is wonderful, in theory, to be "appropriate" in our essays! We want readers to approve of us, and being "inappropriate" for its own sake may alienate them.

But if you worry that it may be inappropriate to express something in your essay, it might be useful to think about how you'd feel if you read an essay by someone else expressing something similar. Would you welcome that writer's difficult story or strong emotions? If you're like most readers, the answer is probably yes; we have much to learn from others' difficult emotions. But it can be scary to tell your *own* difficult stories, even if you want to. It's fine if you decide to change your mind and shift your topic. But if you want to go for it, trying out an unexpected form might help.

For example, if you're angry about something you might try framing your personal essay about your feeling as a **rant**. If you use that title, as in, "The Food in the Cafeteria: A Rant," or "A Rant on Being the Youngest Sister in My Family," the reader will expect you to exaggerate your emotion, perhaps in a humorous way.

Another way you can present strong emotions is *by alternating emotional outbursts with thoughtful self-analysis*: "Why did that bother me so much? I think it might have something to do with my childhood experiences of ... but as I think about it, I understand that my feeling was ..."

You could also experiment with *jumping out of the narrative to address the reader*. For example, you could insert comments like, "you're probably thinking I was overreacting," or "yes, I know I was really out of control, and ...," or "as I write this, I'm worried about how you'll react, because ..."

Students whose drafts seem flat and lifeless sometimes say, "I didn't want to make readers think my experience was too sad. I mean, I'm fine now." It might be true that things are "not that bad" now because you have moved beyond a difficult experience, but minimizing the pain of that experience could squelch the drama of the story you want to tell.

When readers sense that you are honest, they'll trust you as a narrator and view your experience in its own context. They'll want you to describe your emotions in all their power and will find your doing so to be perfectly appropriate.

PUBLISHED EXAMPLE
"Hateful Things"—A Rant

In her secret diary—later known as The Pillow Book—*Sei Shōnagon, a court lady for Empress Fujiwara no Teishi in eleventh-century Japan, wrote a passage called "Hateful Things," which we could see as her version of a somewhat playful "rant" essay. Here's an excerpt with a few of the things she finds hateful:*

One has gone to bed and is about to doze off when a mosquito appears, announcing himself in a reedy voice. One can actually feel the wind made by his wings and, slight though it is, one finds it hateful in the extreme ... One is telling a story about old times when someone breaks in with a little detail that he happens to know, implying that one's own version is inaccurate—disgusting behavior! (25)

PUBLISHED EXAMPLE
Boarding School Memories

Being deeply serious about painful emotions can be very powerful in a personal essay. For example, in, "Such, Such Were the Joys," George Orwell describes his experiences at boarding school. At around age eight he was beaten by the headmaster for wetting his bed. Afterwards, he told classmates that it didn't hurt so much and was sent back to the headmaster's office for a much harder beating. Here is how he tells the reader about his emotions afterwards—how would you judge the "appropriateness" of his expression of pain?

I had fallen into a chair, weakly sniveling. I remember that this was the only time throughout my boyhood when a beating actually reduced me to tears, and curiously enough I was not even now crying because of the pain. The second beating had not hurt very much either. Fright and shame seemed to have anesthetized me. I was crying partly because I felt that this was expected of me, partly from genuine repentance, but partly also because of a deeper grief which is peculiar to childhood and not easy to convey: a sense of desolate loneliness and helplessness, of being locked up not only in a hostile world but in a world of good and evil where the rules were such that it was actually not possible for me to keep them. (272)

Writing Your Conclusion

You might have the impulse to conclude your personal essay with some kind of "here's the moral of the story" statement. However, readers of personal essays are rarely looking for conclusions like that. Say you wrote an essay about getting in trouble for not doing your homework. The obvious conclusion that it's best to always do your homework could fall flat. What if, for example, you ended with the fact that now, years later, your stomach still twists up when homework is assigned? That could make for a more effective conclusion, giving closure without being too heavy-handed.

Here are a few ideas for conclusions to personal essays:

- *Pull the original thread, with a twist.* Example: "I always thought I was right to do what I did, but I see now that it's because I always ignored that little voice in me that knew the truth from the beginning." Or, "suddenly, I detested the design on that supposedly beautiful bowl I'd thought I loved."
- *Look back from the vantage point of your current self.* "Three years later, I look back on that experience and realize that ..." Or "If I had only had more compassion for myself, I would have been able to see that ..." Or "If the current me could have talked to my younger self, I would have said ..."
- *Reflect on how you would have seen your story when you were younger.* Example: "When I was eight I was fascinated by _____, little did I know that it would turn into ..." Or "little did my stubborn twelve-year-old self imagine that one day I would totally disagree with her about ..."
- *Bring in another story from your life that comes to mind in relation to the story you told.* Example: "Oddly enough, I had a very different experience six months later, when ..." Or "And yet, sometimes my reaction to being disagreed with was very different, for example when ..."
- *Bring in a generalization that takes something in your story beyond your individual experience.* Example: after a story about losing your soccer game, reflect on the idea of loss in general and how it has affected people in another context.
- *Make a connection between your own story and an idea or story in the public sphere.* Example: after writing about your relationship with your father, conclude with a reflection about how it connects with a father/son relationship you read about, saw in a film, heard about in a song, etc.

Once you write your conclusion, go back to the beginning of the essay and read through to make sure that the scaffolding holds up. That might mean "planting the seed of your thread" in your introductory paragraphs or making some changes in the rest of the essay to make everything clear.

Writing your conclusion could also open you up to possibilities for even more writing, some of which could end up working well as part of your essay as a whole. Do you have time? If so, it can be interesting to shift the body of your essay around more dramatically to include the interesting ideas that arise when you thought you were working toward the end.

However, maybe you really are out of time. That's okay too: sometimes you simply have to say "no" to making further changes and adding new ideas, and be satisfied with writing a short, nifty conclusion instead. In the process, you may have gathered some notes and possibilities for your next personal essay!

Dress Up Your Personal Essay for the Reading Public

When your essay seems finished to you, take responsibility for it by **reading it aloud.** Questions to consider:

- *Do you stumble over some sentences?* If so, maybe they need fixing?
- *Does any part of your essay make you cringe?* Is that because something in it needs to be changed?
- *Can you clearly follow your line of thinking throughout?* Maybe you need more transitions, or to delete unnecessary sections?
- *Is each paragraph coherent, and a satisfying length?* One-sentence paragraphs, or overly long ones, can be dramatic and useful if they are deliberate, but they're distracting if you put them together carelessly.
- *Are your grammar and spelling correct?* Your essay is not fully finished until they are. If you aren't sure, ask someone for help.

MAIN ASSIGNMENT

Revise, Add Texture To, and Finish Your Personal Essay

As you go back to your draft, reflect on how you can use any of the options above to make it an essay only you can write. Can you give it some extra pizzazz that makes you feel proud when you read it? That means making sure that your essay works as a satisfying whole, clearly leading the reader somewhere from beginning to end; it also might mean strengthening your scenes and the language of your descriptions. Let your essay shine!

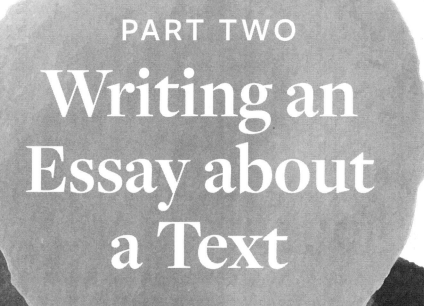

PART TWO

Writing an Essay about a Text

On Reading and Writing about Texts

The Best Way to Become a Better Writer Is to Read

Some students come to college thinking that when they read an assigned text once, they either "get it" or not, period. That's not true! Just as writing well requires revising, *reading well requires re-reading*. If a sentence or passage isn't clear to you, reread it!

You might approach readings with one principal question in mind: "Do I like it?" That's a good start, but only a start—as you'll see in this chapter, you can benefit from asking many other questions as well. Get into the habit of writing down your questions and observations as you read—they are useful not only for understanding what you read, but also for gathering material you might later incorporate into an essay.

I also encourage you to approach any text you read as your teacher. Pay attention to what it shows you, first about how it works in its genre, and then about what it shows you about how *you* would like to write, or would prefer *not* to write.

EXERCISE 1
Who Are You As a Reader?

Answer at least three of the questions below in writing and share them with a peer or your professor:

- What is your relationship with reading?
- What kind of reading do you like best? Least?
- What kind of reading do you do that is not assigned?
- Where do you like to be while reading?
- What is your process when faced with something to read?
- What have you read that you loved? What drew you to it?
- What have you read that you hated? What bothered you about it?
- Can you think of something you read that surprised you?
- If you could write any book, what would it be like?

EXERCISE 2
Do You Find Some Readings Boring?

....

- Can you think of an example of a boring text, or of the types of texts that bore you?
- If so, why do you think that is?
- What associations do texts like it have for you?
- What do you think of their subject(s)?
- What thoughts arise in you as you confront them?

... Open any novel. What is there? Black marks—signs—on white paper. First, they are silent. They are lifeless, lacking signification until the consciousness of the reader imbues them with meaning, allowing a fictitious character like the nameless protagonist of Ralph Ellison's *Invisible Man*, say, to emerge powerfully from the monotonous rows of ebony type. This magical act is, of course, achieved through a concentration, as one reads, and an act of self-surrender that allows an entire fictional world to appear ... (Johnson 39)

I like the way this passage points to the beautiful mystery of reading. Yes, reading requires concentration, and recent studies show that reading on paper can develop our abilities to concentrate better in a world with so many distractions. But Johnson also brings in self-surrender, which gives me pause: Do I surrender myself when I read? Do you? What exactly does Johnson mean by surrender?

I'm not entirely sure, but I find it interesting to try to imagine what he means. Is it that when I read I must put my own ideas aside, at least for a while—to surrender them—in order to be open to what a writer is saying to me?

I think so. And yet at the same time Johnson also says that I'm the one, as a reader, who "imbues meaning" to the words on the page. So do I change the text by imbuing my own meaning but then open myself to be marked by the meaning that lies in what I read? I think that's what Johnson means, because later in the same paragraph he says, "... the electrifying figures and situations Ellison has created reward us richly by *returning our subjective feelings to us transformed*, refined, and alchemized by language into a new vision with the capacity to change our lives forever" (39; italics mine).

To Johnson, then, we let go of our self, or our "subjective feelings," for a while when we read, but in doing so, we allow ourselves to be transformed by what we read. The "new vision" we get changes our lives. Have you ever had an experience like that with reading?

Whether you have or not, reading a text is a complicated and interesting experience, and it is always determined by who you are as a reader. No two people read, or write about, a text in exactly the same way because we all bring our unique set of experiences to our reading.

What Is a Text, and What Does It Mean to Read It?

In this book I'm talking about written texts like books and articles, but the word "text" can certainly also refer to images, film, videos, graphs, and other such media. Even a tree can be a text if you "read" it a certain way. An arborist reads the tree one way; a painter may read it another.

Teachers often complain that students don't read enough. You've probably heard comments like these: "they just pick up the gist of what a text is about from class discussion," "if they read at all, they just skim!" "they rely on plot summaries they find online," or "it's all the fault of their phones!"

To an extent, teachers have a point, no? Before smart phones, if you stepped onto a bus, train, or plane you would have seen many people, students or not, fully engaged in reading newspapers, magazines, or books. Now, it's true, people may be reading books on those phones, or listening to texts via earpods, but many are simply playing games, or scrolling aimlessly through random feeds. Can books or other written texts possibly compete with that steady stream of unexpected, new material?

I think they can, and my goal is to encourage you to love reading and writing about what you read.

As you know, students have a wide range of attitudes toward reading. Some already do respect books and reading, very much. They find it heartbreaking that many of their peers resist reading. Maybe you yourself are already an avid reader, excited about the fact that college requires so much reading and writing.

Or maybe you're someone who would never pick up a book for pleasure because there are so many other ways to be engaged by people and ideas. Maybe you've never had any reason to read a book unless you absolutely had to.

Whatever your thoughts on reading are right now, I'm here to encourage you to read, and write about reading, in a way that has meaning for yourself, not just for your professors.

I see reading as intimate and beautiful because it allows us to get into the heads of writers and learn how they think. Like deep conversations with friends, reading engages us with writers from arenas and mindsets that we might otherwise have no access to. It enriches our thinking, making us surrender our own closed attitudes about the world as we expand the scope of who we are.

Sometimes when I feel inspired by a reading, students tell me that it bores them, or deals with subjects they are not interested in. They might think the author is pompous or annoying, or that the writing is too dense and they just don't get it.

I can't help feeling frustrated that they see the world differently from the way I do. But I've also come to appreciate students' honesty about what they dislike in a text, because their genuine responses have the potential to be effective starting points for their interpretations of a reading. The problem is not that they don't "get" it—that's a reaction we all have at times. It's that they give up on the reading too soon.

The key to reading well is to be patient and give the text time to speak to you. If you don't "get" it at first, challenge yourself to reread and look deeper. Doing so is a way to exercise your brain, deepen your intellect, and make your thinking more sophisticated.

"The Author Repeats the Same Thing Over and Over"

"We got it the first time!" my students sometimes say about a text, "Why do they have to go on and on about the same thing? It's boring!" Yes: when you read a somewhat dense argument, or especially when you skim it, the writer can seem to be unnecessarily repetitive. However, it's extremely rare for essays to get published, not to mention assigned in your class, if the authors are doing nothing but repeating the same argument over and over! Chances are that the writer is in fact developing an idea, and each example adds another angle to their overall plan.

If you think examples in a text are repetitive, look more closely: What does each one contribute differently toward advancing the writer's perspective? Maybe the answer is nothing, which is a flaw in the text. But more likely, you'll discover that writers choose multiple examples for good reasons.

Uncovering how they do that will help you work with examples in your own writing.

Appreciating details of a text you read might require going back to re-read sections, or to discuss a scene in detail with a friend, noting places where you have questions. Posing those questions—to yourself, your professor, and your classmates—will help you clarify your reading.

As you follow an author's argument, it's useful to apply inward-looking techniques as well. Your own reactions, when you take time to examine them, can lead you toward writing an essay only you can write about the text.

To Read Well, Pay Attention to Nuances

"Nuance" is one of the first words I make sure all my students know in their first college semester. Many of them don't know it at first, so I write the definition on the board.

"Nuance"

1. "A subtle or slight variation or difference in meaning, expression, feeling, etc.
2. A subtle shade of a basic colour; a slight difference or variation in shade or tone.
3. A delicate gradation or subtle alteration in musical expression." (*Oxford English Dictionary*)

If you can become engaged by nuance, you'll become a better reader, writer, and thinker. Not only that, you'll become a more interesting person. Imagine that you are walking out of a movie with a friend. You found the movie disturbing, but you aren't entirely sure why. As you walk out, you ask, "What did you think of the movie?"

"It was good," says your friend.

"I thought that woman's whole life was so strange!" you answer. "Why didn't she want to leave her apartment? Wasn't it odd that she started crying just because her son pet the dog?"

"Yeah. I have to get to my homework now—gotta go."

Before your friend leaves, would you like to hear more about their reaction? Of course you would! You want to explore the nuances with them that will help you understand the movie in more depth. By being unwilling to respond to your thoughts and questions, or to dig into their own reactions to the "text" of the movie, your friend is an unsatisfying reader: unwilling to take the time to look at nuances of the "text" of the movie.

Let's dig deeper: first into reading, then into writing about what you read, and finally into what reading can teach you about structuring your own essays.

We All Read Texts Differently

What exactly does it mean to read a text? The answer is not as obvious as you might think.

Students sometimes come to college assuming that everyone reads any text basically the same way: we all look at the words on the page and draw fairly similar conclusions, right? Actually, wrong. We all bring *different* attitudes and experiences to our reading, which makes each person's reading unique. But how about something like a math textbook, you might ask, wouldn't everyone read a text like *that* the same way? It just tells you how to solve the problems. Simple, right?

Not necessarily. If you look closely even at a math textbook you may find that various people read it differently. One person might love the author's tone and feel that she's explaining it exactly as they like, but another might be put off by her method and have trouble grasping her discussion of the problems. Their reactions depend on their previous experiences and their ways of understanding mathematical concepts. The same is true for textbooks in other STEM (science, technology, engineering, and mathematics) classes, as well as those in other disciplines. No one book works the same way for everyone, and even experts in a given field have readings of colleagues' books that vary widely.

Have you found that some authors offer explanations in a way that enables you to grasp concepts well, while others seem unnecessarily confusing to you even if your friend is happy with them? If so, don't worry; you're not alone.

Interpreting a Text

You might have had a teacher who presented a poem to you and wanted you to come up with the one "answer" that conformed to his reading of it. That teacher might have been influenced by critics and his own professors, and by the time he was teaching you he was convinced that only one interpretation was correct. If you noticed something unusual about the poem and offered a different sort of angle, he might have dismissed your reading as "wrong." Chances are, though, that there's a literary critic somewhere who has an interpretation that contradicts the one your teacher thought was airtight.

You might also have had a teacher on the other extreme from the strict poetry teacher, who told you that "anything goes" when you interpret poems.

"Whatever you think the poem is about is fine," that teacher might have said, "since we all see the world differently. You can get whatever you want from any poem; it doesn't even matter what the poet had in mind."

But the extremes of "only *this* interpretation is valid" on one side and "anything goes" on the other are both problematic. They can lead us to think it's impossible to interpret texts productively on our own. That attitude could push us to become fed up with *all* conversations in which there are disagreements, concluding that they involve each side only producing evidence to support their own ideas, with no hope that people with conflicting opinions could talk to each other productively.

However, academic study, and in particular learning to interpret texts, can offer you much more. It helps you develop skills for exchanging ideas with others in a thoughtful and productive search for reality and truth, not only about texts but about the world.

A first step in learning to interpret a text can be to seek clarity about **the framework you personally bring to a reading**. That means *digging into your reasons* for the likes, dislikes, and conclusions you draw when you read. The next step is to look for **evidence**, both from the text and from your own experience, to back up your thinking. The more you understand your own perspectives and where they came from, the more proficient you can be as an interpreter.

Let's say your friend tells you a movie is "terrible," for example. You most likely will decide whether to see it based on what you know of your friend's framework for approaching movies. Maybe your friend hates anything that has to do with guns, and the movie is about mafia struggles in which people shoot each other. If you happen to *like* mafia movies you'd need to hear more. "What makes it terrible?" you might ask. "Is it the fact that people shoot each other a lot?" If your friend says yes, you know that unlike them you might enjoy the movie. But maybe your friend says, "Beyond the guns, there was no psychological insight. I had no idea why the characters behaved as they did—they were just pretty people doing inexplainable things." In that case, they are giving you a larger framework for making a more informed decision, based on your own preferences. If you value character development, your friend's interpretation might lead you to decide against watching the movie.

When you know someone well, then, you know whether what they like in a movie is similar, or not, to what you like, and that knowledge gives you a *framework* for reacting to the evidence they bring you from their "reading" of movies. In other words, you have been interpreting frameworks much longer than you might think.

Developing interpretations of academic texts is not so different from "reading" your friends and their attitudes. Pay attention to your reactions!

What makes an interpretation of a text valid? *First and foremost, evidence!* The best away to prove the legitimacy of your interpretation is to back it up with specific references to the text. If you tell me that a poem I think is just about baseball is in fact about love, I might dismiss your idea completely. However, if you can point to some specific elements of that poem—a reference to "embracing" the bat, say, or the "many delights" of throwing the ball—I will want to hear more because you will open my mind to new possibilities of interpretation.

"Evidence"

When you write about a text, the evidence for what you say comes from quotations from the text, references to specific points the author made, and/or data given by the author—graphs, charts, tables, etc. Your evidence is there to back up whatever you have to say about the text.

Gather Evidence As You Read

Evidence is the wheel driving academic work, from science to humanities. You wouldn't want someone to give you medicine without evidence that it works, and that means they must do many experiments to gather information about it. You don't want to travel on a bridge made by scientists who did not ensure that the evidence they relied on for construction was one hundred percent legitimate. You might not even want to take someone's view of a movie seriously—would you?—if they did not give you any specific evidence for their views.

To get people to trust your position on a text, explain how the evidence supports that position. Even if someone does not agree with you, your evidence will help them understand why and how you see the text the way you do.

Here's a method I often hear beginning students say they follow when they write an essay on a text: "Think of a thesis, write the essay, and then find some quotes to plug in to back the thesis up." Does that sound like a decent approach? As a high school student, I might have thought so. But my advice to you now is *do not do it!*

Why not? Because it defeats the whole purpose of writing about a text! Evidence should *lead* you to your conclusion, not the other way around! Your essay will be far more interesting, not to mention convincing, when you gather evidence first and draw conclusions afterwards.

Too many students, faced with a writing assignment on a text, will read or skim through the text, close the book, and then, maybe a day or two later, sit in front of a blank page or screen, hoping for inspiration and fretting that they have no idea what to write. If they haven't taken steps toward the essay other than wracking their brains for a thesis, or maybe looking through class notes for anything that might seem like an argument, it's no wonder if they aren't sure what to say.

What those students miss is how much the text can work *with* them. Finding an approach to your assignment that grows out of specific places in the text does not happen magically after you read, it should begin *while you are reading*.

If you let it, any text you read gives you plenty of material for formulating an essay about it if you read closely, paying attention to your own reactions and questions.

One of the best, and easiest, ways to begin gathering evidence and generating an interpretation of a text is by freewriting about it. Pause periodically while reading, and write, without planning, about your text. Bring in any observations or questions you have—your freewrite is not an essay, of course, but it can be invaluable in helping you generate ideas for one.

STUDENT EXAMPLE
Scott Russell Sanders and Religion

In this student's freewrite about reading Scott Russell Sanders's essay called, "Under the Influence," he is using writing to explore his own puzzlement about why Sanders would talk about religion so much in an essay about his father's drunkenness. These ideas are leading the student to an essay—he's not yet sure exactly what he wants to say on the topic, but he'll get there by continuing to write. Though most readers of this essay focus on the alcoholism of Sanders' father, this student keeps going back to the issue of religion, which is important to him from his own experience. His honesty about that enriches his interpretation.

I was intrigued by the fact that Scott Russell Sanders chose to mention religion so frequently in this essay. It is clear from the text that he went to Sunday School as a youth, but it is unclear how big a part of his life religion is to him now. He makes an interesting comparison between his alcoholic, distant, and abusive father and the different figures in what many consider a holy and sacred text. Many times people turn to religion not to gain a new perspective, but to find justification for beliefs that they already hold. Elements of this could be present in the way Sanders regards his dad. Maybe he is turning to religion so that he doesn't feel as alone when he considers the difficult upbringing he had. Or maybe he compares his father to biblical figures as a means to believing that his dad was more a victim of his circumstances than an inherently immoral human being. (GK)

MAIN ASSIGNMENT

Making Sense of a Difficult Text (in five parts)

As a prelude to writing a longer essay about a text, let's try an exercise aimed at demonstrating how writing can help you gather evidence about a challenging reading.

We'll be working with just one paragraph of a difficult text, *Gender Trouble* by Judith Butler.

PART **1**: GATHER BACKGROUND
BEFORE READING

It might help you to know that Judith
Butler is a philosopher and theorist of
gender. Even sophisticated readers find
her theories, and her prose, to be complex and sometimes difficult. But also very
interesting!

As you approach the following passage,
you should be aware of two different, con-
tradictory ways of looking at human gender
identity:

- "Biology as destiny": the belief that
  everyone is born as one sex, male or
  female, that completely defines their gender identity
- "Gender is socially constructed": the belief that no matter what biolog-
  ical sex we have at birth, the social experiences we have—as opposed
  to the body we are born into—"construct," and are thus the source of,
  our gender identity.

In this passage, Butler explores nuances of the second concept of socially
constructed gender.

PART **2**: READ BUTLER'S PASSAGE

Read the following passage more than once, underlining parts that strike
you, taking notes as you go, and freewriting about each of the following
questions—there are no wrong answers:

- What intrigues you about this passage? Why?
- Do part(s) of it seem to push you away? Why?
- What does this passage make you think or wonder about?

PUBLISHED EXAMPLE

From **Gender Trouble** *by Judith Butler*

Is there "a" gender which persons are set to have, or is it an essential attribute that a person is said to be, as implied in the question "what gender are you?" When feminist theories claim that gender is the cultural interpretation of sex or that gender is culturally constructed, what is the manner or mechanism of this construction? If gender is constructed, could it be constructed differently, or does its constructedness imply some form of social determinism, foreclosing the possibility of agency and transformation? Does "construction" suggest that certain laws generate gender differences along universal axes of sexual difference? How and where does the construction of gender take place? What sense can we make of a construction that cannot assume a human constructor prior to that construction? On some accounts, the notion that gender is constructed suggests a certain determinism of gender meanings inscribed on anatomically differentiated bodies, where those bodies are understood as passive recipients of an inexorable cultural law. When the relevant "culture" that "constructs" gender is understood in terms of such a law or set of laws, then it seems that gender is as determined and fixed as it was under the biology-is-destiny formulation. In such a case, not biology, but culture, becomes destiny. (10–11)

PART ❸: WITH A PARTNER, SHARE YOUR NOTES, AND GO FURTHER

- Choose a sentence in the passage that you both agree is especially significant to you.
- Choose another sentence that you think is significant to Butler.
- What confuses or alienates you in this text? Can you say why?
- Choose one idea in the passage and explain in your own words what you think Butler is saying, including any questions you have.
- Can you agree on an opinion about that idea? What evidence from the passage backs up that opinion?

PART **4**: SHARE YOUR IDEA AND EVIDENCE WITH ONE OR TWO
OTHER PAIRS OF STUDENTS, OR WITH THE WHOLE CLASS

- Note similarities and differences in your approaches.
- Does anything you hear change or enhance your thinking?

PART **5**: READ THE PASSAGE AGAIN

- Write about, and/or discuss, what you understand now about the text
  that you didn't on your first reading.

* * *

After doing this assignment, you can understand how writing about a text
might help you move toward increasing understanding. You can also probably see that sharing ideas with other people, as academics do often, helps
you deepen your thinking. (You might even be inspired to learn more about
Butler and/or other theories of gender!) You can follow the same practice
with your assigned essay about a text.

Read and Respond to Your Assigned Text

Read, Write About, and Discuss a Text Assigned by Your Professor (in three parts)

PART **1**: BEFORE READING

Before reading any text, here are some questions to ask:

- What is the text's genre and purpose?
- Who is its audience?
- How is it organized? What do you notice about sections or chapters?
- Who is the writer? Do you know anything about their perspective on the topic?
- When was it written? Do you know anything about its context?

PART ❷: WRITE WHILE READING

The writing you do while reading is the beginning of the process of forming your interpretation of the text, with the quotes you choose as evidence.

Take notes: While reading a text you plan to write about, keep a notebook or computer nearby as you read, and occasionally stop to write down your first impressions and questions while reading. If you own the text, you might mark sections or passages, writing reactions and questions in the margins.

Do freewrites: Stop reading when you have a noteworthy reaction to the text, time yourself for five minutes, and write as though you are talking about the reading to a friend. Don't plan in advance, just follow any idea that occurs to you, no matter how odd; don't worry about whether it's "correct." Be honest with yourself—it's no problem if your reactions seem negative or wrong—just get them out. If you have conflicting ideas, write about the contradictions. No one but you has to read these. They are a painless way to gather material useful for your essay; you might even be able to pull sentences from your freewrites to put in your eventual draft.

Some moments when you could stop to write notes:

- You like something the author said.
- You find something in the text annoying.
- Something the author said reminds you of something else.
- You have a question.
- You're skipping through a whole page without really reading it. Why? Reread to find out.
- You want to go back and reread something later, maybe because you love it, or maybe because you think it will make more sense once you've read the rest.
- A reaction is forming in your mind that could work well for your assignment. Write it down, even if you don't know how it might work.

Gather Quotes: Choosing quotes and writing about them while reading, instead of trying to find them afterward, will help you to have the *evidence* that will lead you to what you want to say about the text. When you find a passage in the text you think could be interesting to quote in your essay, you might include it in your notes as follows:

- Copy at least some of the quote, and/or page numbers or links to help you find it
- Write a sentence or two about what you hear the author saying in the quote, as well as your own thoughts and reactions

- Write your questions or confusions about it
- Make connections between the quote and other parts of the text, or other texts

PART **3**: SHARE IDEAS ABOUT THE TEXT

A good way to move toward writing about a text is to discuss it with others. In discussions about the text—in small groups, in a whole-class discussion, or one on one, you can revise and develop your interpretations of your text. Hearing others' views might change your mind; it might also reinforce the thoughts you were already developing. Be open to rethinking and deepening your ideas as you share them with peers and your professor.

Write Your Essay about a Text

"Thesis"

A statement of a *topic with an attitude about the topic*. Most academic essays require that you present a thesis and provide evidence to back it up.

- "Toni Morrison's novel *Beloved*," isn't a thesis, it's a topic.
- "Morrison's novel, *Beloved*, gets readers to appreciate how an unthinkable act can become an ethical choice for an enslaved woman," is a thesis.

A general rule is that a thesis should be **arguable**, meaning that someone might productively disagree with you, with evidence, after which you could counter-argue with evidence of your own. You can't argue with "Toni Morrison's novel *Beloved*," but you could argue about whether her character's act is an ethical choice.

Types of Thesis-and-Proof Essays

Here are some ways your professor might ask you to write a thesis-driven essay about a text. They all require that you use evidence from the text to "prove" or "demonstrate" your thesis.

Type 1: Completely Open

- Come up with a thesis about your chosen text and write a clear argument to prove it.
- White a thesis that compares two (or more) texts.

Type 2: Respond to a Specific Question

- What is the relationship between the main character and her mother?
- Analyze how the text serves as an example of one of the rhetorical concepts we studied earlier in the semester.

> ### "Analyze"
>
> The word "analyze" can mean different things in assignments. It always involves examining something to explore the nuances of its components, but for some professors it might mean developing an argument about those components by proving a thesis; for others it might mean simply noting the parts of something. Make sure you know what your professors mean when they use the words "analyze" or "analysis."

Type 3: Compare This Reading to Something Else

- To another text: How does this novel explore class differences compared to the way that play does?
- To another author: How might T.S. Eliot view this novel?
- Through the lens of a concept: Apply Marx's economic perspective to this article's analysis.

Type 4: Personal Reaction

- Based on your own **reading**: How did Lopate's essay make you feel about New York City?
- Based on the text's **ideas**: How have your thoughts about your relationship to activism evolved after reading this text?
- Departing from the text: Inspired by anything you read in the text, write a personal narrative, driven by a thesis.

Type 5: Close Reading

- Do a **formal** close reading, sometimes called a "précis": Give the reader a clear summary of what the author is doing in some part of the text; this assignment may or may not require a thesis.
- Do a **personal** close reading: Look in detail at a passage and explore your own thinking about it. I did a personal close reading at the start of Chapter 4 when I described my thinking about Johnson's text. My thesis was that the idea of "surrendering while reading" is paradoxical.

Move toward Your Essay (in Six Steps)

When you begin constructing the draft of your essay, make sure you have a clear idea of your assignment. If not, ask your professor for clarification. Remember that when you write about a text *readers expect* that you let them know what evidence—quotes and references to the text—led you to your interpretation.

With your assignment in mind, including its suggested length, gather your reading notes and freewrites, along with the text you're writing about. If you don't yet have enough freewrites and notes, go back to the text, choose some places in it that you find thought provoking and/or that speak directly to your assignment, and write about them.

Your freewrites and notes might seem like a mess of diverging fragments of topics, but most likely there is plenty in that "mess" that can be useful to you. The following strategies might help.

Step 1: Read Through Your Freewrites and Reading Notes

- Underline or mark ideas or moments that interest you.
- If your assignment is specific, what perspective on it is starting to emerge? What stories or other ideas, including contradictions, might help you address the assignment?
- If the assignment is more open, what potential overall idea or impression arises for you that could lead to an effective thesis about the text, based on the assignment?

Step 2: Review the Text as a Whole with Your Own Ideas in Mind

- Reread the opening paragraphs of the text. What do you see about the author's framework?
- Skip to the conclusion. Reread it, reflecting on what has changed from beginning to end in terms of the writer's ideas, attitudes, or style.
- Step back and take a bird's-eye view of the whole text. What do you notice about its overall structure? Are there headings, images, charts? If so, how do they contribute to what the overall text is doing, and to your thinking?
- Will your essay be about the text as a whole, or just one part?
- Reread a **chosen quote** in its larger context, beginning at least a few paragraphs before the quote and continuing beyond it. What opinion or

idea is it expressing, either on its own or in the context of your assignment, and how does it connect to your own thinking and freewrites?
- Take note: What do you see that you had not noticed before?
- Repeat the process with other quotes you've marked while reading.

Step 3: Generate a Working Thesis

With your assignment in mind, bring in your critical muscle to reread your notes and decide on a working thesis about your text.

You might work in conversation with a classmate or someone else. It can be useful to have another person ask questions to help you clarify and organize your own thinking.

> ### "Working Thesis"
> A working thesis is a preliminary thesis that you use to draft your essay. It's called "working" because you are open to changing or tweaking it as you develop your ideas.

Here are some questions to ask, either on your own or with a peer, on your way to a working thesis.

- If your assignment is open, what parts of the text spoke to you the most as you read? Why do you think that is?
- If you're working with a specific question from your professor, how do your preliminary ideas address it?
- Did an idea or opinion recur more than once in your notes and freewrites?
- Is there something you wonder about or don't quite understand about the text? Don't ignore it—exploring your question or confusion can be the start of an excellent thesis.

Here's how your working thesis might evolve before you even start writing:

- You might find that the first working thesis you came up with is too broad, and you need to *narrow it down* to something much more specific. "The essay is about all the different kinds of empathy," let's say, might become, "the essay questions how much self-interest plays a role in empathy."
- You might decide you're focusing on something too narrow and need to *expand your scope.* "I will look at the significance of one paragraph in the novel," might become, "chapter three is the most important chapter, because ..."

Step 4: Give Texture to Your Working Thesis

Sometimes you might decide on a working thesis but find that it seems bland to you. There are ways to make it snappier!

For example, instead of dismissing parts of your idea that don't seem to fit, you might dig into contradictions you see in the text. Let's say you're reading a poem and wondering if the horse in it is supposed to be a metaphor. You might come up with a working thesis like this:

> The horse works as a metaphor in this poem, representing the joys of freedom.

That statement invites you to write an essay in which you list all the descriptions of the horse in the poem, explaining the aspects of freedom that it represents. As you do so, you might notice that in some descriptions, later in the poem, the horse does not seem joyful at all! "Oh no!" you might think. "I got it all wrong, and must start all over again with an entirely different working thesis!"

That might be true, but more often, doubts about your working thesis can lead you to interesting nuances. For example, you could let your thesis evolve to this:

> Some may see the horse as a metaphor for the joys of freedom; however, the horse's increasing sadness emphasizes the danger of a painful kind of freedom that results from having no boundaries.

That's what I'd call a more textured—complex—thesis.

Faced with a contradiction to their working thesis, some students think they have to choose one side and abandon the other. But a contradiction can be gold, because it adds a layer of complexity. Don't resist a thesis that moves away from "X means Y" to something like, "at first X and Y seem similar, but in fact Z complicates their connection, because ..."

Another way to give texture to your working thesis can be to mention how it echoes something you have observed elsewhere. You might realize, for example, that one of your freewrites grew out of something you didn't think of writing about: a long talk with a friend, a movie or show you saw, a question you had in another class, another reading, etc. Sometimes bringing that external idea into your essay can liven it up.

In other words, discover and build your thesis not out of empty air, but by exploring the thinking that happened, and continues to happen, as you read and reread the text!

If you are writing in response to a specific assignment, keep that assignment in mind throughout your reading, note-taking, and drafting process. Before writing your draft, reread or skim the text again with the assignment in mind, looking for more evidence.

For example, let's say your assignment is to read a text *through the lens of* another author or idea.

This kind of assignment asks you to imagine how someone, usually another author, might view your text. The first step for such an assignment is to make sure you understand what the person (or idea) whose lens you should be looking through would say. If you don't, you have to find out. Go back to your notes or do research. Otherwise, trying to write your draft will plunge you into a difficult swamp.

Say the assignment is to read your text through the lens of what Freud would say about that poem about a horse; the first step might be to understand Freud's theory that childhood experiences determine future actions. You might ask yourself,

What do I think Freud would say about that horse? Maybe it connects to what we read about the Oedipus complex? Could the horse somehow represent the poet's father?

And then you're on your way to a thesis.

At the start of constructing your essay, let any thesis you have in mind be a "working thesis"—you can't be sure yet how it will evolve once you start writing. Pick any idea from your free writes or notes that can potentially be a working thesis, even if you don't like it all that much.

Step 5: Once You Have a Working Thesis, Develop Your Essay

You don't have to start with your introduction. In fact, you might defer writing any introduction until you've written the rest of the essay and know exactly what you want to be introducing.

Remember, quotes and other references to the text are not a last-minute add-on—*they are the fuel for your essay*. The best way to start constructing your draft might be to go straight to the passage or idea in the text that you find most interesting or challenging. Start writing about how it engages your working thesis. You can figure out later where that writing fits best in your essay as a whole.

In other words, feel free to write your draft in pieces that you will arrange later into an order that works for you.

Make sure you are reading any quote you write about in context—read the passages before and after it. And *don't let your quote do all the work* on its own: take time to explain its context to the reader and say briefly in your own words what *you* think it's saying, and how it speaks to your working-thesis idea. "This loving, detailed description of the horse leads the reader to view it as a positive force in the poem." Keep in mind that your readers will not read the text under discussion the same way you do. Explain how the evidence you've chosen supports your own point of view.

Step 6: Continue to Write Your Draft

After writing everything you have to say about one important passage or idea, go back to your working thesis. Does it still work? If it does, find another section of the text that helps you develop your idea further, and proceed. If it doesn't, find a thesis that better reflects the direction you're going in.

Here are more questions you can ask yourself from time to time while developing your draft:

- What's working well in this draft so far? Why?
- What isn't working? Why?
- Does my working thesis still work? If not, how can I tweak it?
- What else can I do to make this essay work better?

Writing Your Introduction

Whenever you feel ready to write your introduction, consider beginning with a quote, a story, a general reflection, or whatever makes sense for your essay.

It's usually a good idea to make *a clear statement of your thesis* as part of your introduction. The *first sentence* of your essay might be the best place to do so. Another common convention is for your thesis to be the *last sentence of your first paragraph*. If you begin with an anecdote or other story it could be fine to save your thesis for the *second* or *third paragraph*. And if you want to lead the reader through some steps before letting them know what your thesis is, you can consider holding off on stating your thesis until the *last paragraph*. The most important thing is that you have a plan for introducing your topic the way you do, and proceed systematically from there. The reader should have an idea, or at least a hint, of where you're going in the essay by the time they get to the end of your introductory remarks. Plant the seed of the thread!

Conventions for Discussing a Text in Your Essay

The first time you mention an author, use their first and last name, along with the title of their work. *After that that use only their last name.* Integrate your references smoothly into your essay. For example:

- "As Ta-Nehisi Coates notes, in 'The Case for Reparations' ..."
- "Coates's point about reparations, on the other hand, is ..."
- "But Coates answers that objection, when he says ..."
- "Some might think that reparations for slavery would be impossible. However, Coates brings up the point that ..."

Put all **direct quotes** from the text in "quotation marks" if they are four lines or less, followed by the author's name (if it is not clear in the text) and a page number or notation of where the text came from in parentheses. If the quote is longer, indent it as a block quote, with no quotation marks, followed by a parenthetical in-text citation according to the rules of the citation system you are using.

Many students come to college thinking there is only one way to cite sources, but in fact there are various systems for doing so, depending on the field you're writing in and your professor's preference.

Most humanities classes require MLA (Modern Language Association) author-page citations in the text (as used in this book) with a "Works Cited" list of all the sources cited (not just quoted) at the end of the essay. However, history and the visual and performing arts usually require the Chicago/Turabian style using footnotes/endnotes with an author-title format and a "Bibliography." Almost all other academic fields use author-date citations in the text and a "References" list of cited sources based on styles such as APA (American Psychological Association) (most social sciences) or IEEE (Institute of Electrical and Electronics Engineers) and similar author-date formats in STEM (science, technology, engineering, and mathematics).

Ask your professor what citation format to use, both for "in-text" citation of quotes, and for the format for your Works Cited list. You can find directions for how to do so online (for example, at Purdue's Online Writing Lab) or by consulting a reference librarian.

Writing Summaries

Writing about a text involves summarizing either the whole or parts of it as you develop your ideas. You might think summarizing is easy: simply tell someone what the text is about, right?

But it can be harder than you think. Many writers get stuck when it comes to summary; they're more comfortable writing their opinion of a text than they are at explaining what's in it.

The two most important components of writing a summary of a text are:

- Providing a clear overview of the text, made up *only of the most important details*
- Leaving yourself out of it to get into the writer's mindset, not your own.

Why is that so hard, and what's hard about it? Imagine that someone you know has seen a movie, and you're wondering whether you'd like to see it too.

"What's it about?" you might ask. In other words, you're asking for a summary. Now imagine that the person says:

> There's this young woman, and she's kind of depressed, but not too bad, and she lives in a really nice house, and she's cooking dinner one night, taking broccoli out of the refrigerator, and her phone rings, and it's a friend and they chat, and meanwhile her cat is rubbing itself against her legs, and she's wearing orange capri pants, and ...

You might want to shout, "Get to the point! These things only happen in the first few minutes!"

"I'm getting there," the person might answer. They might have a genuine desire to tell you the main point, but feel that you will need all these details to understand.

But you won't, because you want an overview. Summarizing means standing back and looking at the big picture, ignoring most of the details. To do it well, you must determine which details are crucial and which are secondary.

Some people who are very detail-oriented, like the person describing the movie above, might be excellent when it comes to remembering and making use of a range of details, but they struggle when it's time to give a quick overview. On the other hand, people who are good at summarizing sometimes get restless and bored when details are important. Are you more like one of those or the other?

The brief descriptions that let a viewer know whether they want to see a movie are a great example of summary: your friend in the hypothetical example above might have summarized the story more effectively as,

> A young secretary's house is broken into, and she ends up becoming friends with the robber. A wild night ensues that changes both their lives for the better.

This summary gives you the gist of the plot, and lets you know whether you might be interested in seeing the movie. You'll learn the rest of the details if you watch it; you don't need them to know whether the movie appeals to you or not. As you know, nearly all movies and books come with such brief summaries—without them, they're virtually impossible to sell. In fact, the whole advertising and public relations industry depends on good summaries. No matter what you do in life, it's in your interest to know how to construct a good summary.

So what's the best way to do it? It depends on how much space you have. You can write a very brief overview:

> In *Frames of Mind*, Howard Gardner describes multiple types of intelligence.

That's a very short summary of a long book, but it gives us the most basic overall facts.

Here's a somewhat longer summary of the book:

> Gardner questions the idea of defining "intelligence" as just one skill. He puts forth the idea that humans have multiple types of intelligence, and he describes each one, with their implications for the field of education and beyond.

In each case, the writing is objective—we don't get a personal sense of who the writer is of either summary. Any reader would summarize any text at least slightly differently, but you can tell a summary is effective when it is recognized as valid by virtually everyone who has read the text.

Of course, you can also write a good summary that does include your personal perspective. For example:

> When I read *Frames of Mind*, I was very surprised. I had always thought that intelligence was one thing, and people were either smart or they weren't. But Gardner's ideas of multiple intelligences got me to see that people can be "intelligent" in different ways. The fact that I'm a dancer means I have a kind of intelligence—he calls it "kinesthetic"—that many people don't have.

While this summary is explicitly personal, it still describes Gardner's book in a way that readers would agree helps give them a good sense of what it's about.

A good way to strengthen your summarizing skills is to practice them. When you read something or watch a movie, try summarizing it to a friend, or just to yourself. After reading a text you will write about, write an instant one-sentence summary of it. That will help you remember what you read, and it will also help your future writing. If you can't summarize your own essay, it's probably not as effective as it should be.

EXERCISE 1

To Practice, Summarize a Section of a Text Your Whole Class Has Read

- Summarize it in *one sentence*.
- Summarize it in a *short paragraph*.
- *Compare your summaries with those of your classmates*, either in groups or simply by reading them aloud to the class. Notice which strategies work better than others.

Paraphrasing Passages

You've most likely heard **paraphrasing** defined as "said in your own words." It is a kind of summary that focuses only on a specific section of text.

The difficulty of paraphrasing is to find a balance between two extremes—on the one hand, your words and sentences should not be too close to the original; on the other, you shouldn't insert too much of your own ideas because that would prevent you from respecting the original.

If I am to paraphrase the paragraph above, here's how I could fall into either extreme:

- *Attempted paraphrase*: It's difficult to paraphrase because the problem is balancing two extremes. On the one hand you shouldn't be too close to the original and on the other you shouldn't move too far from respecting the original.
- *Why the above doesn't work*: It's too similar to the original—it's not a paraphrase, it's simply a poor copy. In an essay, it would probably make more sense to quote directly than to paraphrase this way.

Here's the other extreme:

- *Attempted paraphrase*: It's hard to paraphrase because you can never bring in what *you* have to say. I tried to do that once and it didn't work. It's really hard for me to be objective and leave myself out of it.
- *Why the above doesn't work*: The writer might understand the two extremes, but their presentation of ideas moves too much into their own experience and doesn't give the reader a good sense of the original.

Here's an effective paraphrase of the original paragraph:

> Difficulties with paraphrasing fall into two general, and opposite, categories. One quotes too directly, leaving the writer open to plagiarism charges; the other is too subjective, departing too much from the sense of the original.

EXERCISE 2
Paraphrasing Practice

- With a partner, write a paraphrase of one paragraph of a text you have both read. What do you notice as you negotiate the process?
- Paraphrase a section of the text you plan to quote in your essay and share it with a partner or your class. Does your paraphrase give them a clear idea of the text without sounding too similar to it?

STUDENT EXAMPLE
Combining Paraphrases with the Development of Ideas and Quotes

When you freewrite immediately after reading a text, you might discover that even without trying you include paraphrases as well as personal reflections. For example, here's how a student includes paraphrase and a direct quote while freewriting about his personal response to Anne Lamott's "Shitty First Drafts":

Lamott becomes very sarcastic when she brings up the idea of a writer getting it right on their first try because ... if somebody claims to write perfect first drafts, then they are probably lying or are unrealistic. She says that a first draft should almost look as though a child wrote it, and this is how you will really know if you wrote down all the ideas that you are thinking. Most of the draft can be disregarded ... but ... [o]ne sentence out of the whole draft could end up being the overall idea of the paper. "Just get it all down on paper, because there may be

> something great in those six crazy pages that you would have never gotten to by more rational, grown-up means" (23).
>
> Lamott's work was eye opening for me as a writer and also for my life. When starting something new everyone is going to struggle. Whether it is starting a paper in Lamott's case, or any other new skill in life, it is going to take shitty drafts to get to the finished product. I never thought I would find myself comparing writing a paper for English class to my life but digging into her essay made me think outside the box ... Nobody starts out perfect and it only can get better after the shitty first draft. (CC)

We use summary, paraphrase, and personal reflections in much of what we write. Are you beginning to see the differences between them?

Preventing Plagiarism

> #### "Plagiarism"
> We generally define plagiarism as the practice of using someone else's writing as though you wrote it yourself, without quotation marks or citation.
> **Do not plagiarize! It's a crime in the academic world and beyond.**

Plagiarizing in essays subjects you to severe sanctions by colleges and universities, including suspension or even expulsion. *If you have any doubt about whether you are paraphrasing or citing correctly, ask someone for help.*

There are two overall kinds:

Deliberate Plagiarism: Copying someone else's language, with consciousness that doing so is wrong, and presenting it without citation as though you wrote it yourself. That could mean taking sections from published texts without citing them, or using material written by peers or others, or even by computer bots. There are many ways for instructors to discover this kind of cheating, and the consequences can be severe.

Unintentional Plagiarism: Sometimes a writer plagiarizes without meaning to, either because they don't know the rules of citation, or because they don't know how to paraphrase in a way that makes their words significantly different from those of the original. That might not be punished as severely, but it is still unethical, and usually also punishable. It's up to you to take responsibility for your citations.

Writing Your Conclusion

Your conclusion should refer to the text you've written about and make a final statement about your thesis. You might begin with a summary of the points you've made if it seems appropriate, but a simple repetition of what you said in your introduction probably isn't enough.

For example, you could point to more work that could be done on the issue at hand. Or, if you see a connection between your thesis and something outside the text, that too might be part of your conclusion. Your conclusion points from your essay into the future—use your imagination to write a conclusion only you would write, or if you're stuck, ask for help.

After writing your conclusion, go back to reread the beginning of your essay to make sure that in some way it links clearly with the ending. Does the essay as a whole hold up? Are paragraphs coherent? Do your quotes illustrate what they're supposed to illustrate? Did you cite correctly? Is your conclusion satisfying? If so, pat yourself on the back for completing your draft!

But before you walk away from it, make sure you have cited your texts correctly. Skip a line at the end of your draft, center the words "Works Cited," and list all the sources you've used, alphabetically by author, in the proper form, which you can find online, for example at OWL, Purdue's Online Writing Lab.

MAIN ASSIGNMENT

Write a Draft of a Thesis-and-Proof Essay about Your Text

Using your assigned reading, write a thesis-and-proof essay that contains a clear thesis that you demonstrate with evidence. The work you did in Chapter 5 with your reading will serve as fuel for your essay.

Learn from Other Writers as You Revise Your Draft

Reading Essays Teaches You about Writing Them

During the revision process, it's useful to be particularly attentive to what other writers, including peers, can indirectly teach you about your own writing.

Most students, and most readers in general, approach reading other people's work for the subject alone. Whether reading a math book or a poem, they want information they can use. There's nothing wrong with that, but if you read *only* for information, you might miss out not only on the beauty of language and style, but also on what you can learn about writing from the way other writers write.

Have you noticed that people who dress well tend to look around a lot at other people's outfits? They might get overly critical at times, but they are also continually seeking new possibilities. "The way he knots his scarf looks good," they might think, and then later experiment with knotting their own scarf that way. They note patterns, shapes, and colors, which they may later seek out. Seeing someone looking good with, say, a certain combination of

yellow and turquoise, they might later, even unconsciously, combine those colors in an outfit of their own.

When you approach other people's essays as a writer yourself, you can be engaged in a metaphorical version of "trying on" various types of structures and strategies you can later use in your own writing. Pay attention to how writers present themselves; they will offer new styles you might decide to add to your metaphorical "closet." They can also show you what you *don't* like in an essay's style.

Being the "audience" for another writer's work is one of the best ways to develop an awareness of the way your own readers will be an audience for yours.

What Other Writers Can Give You: New Techniques

Here are some questions you might ask about someone else's text as you read, in order to add to your own "toolbox" for writing essays.

- How does the essay open? How does the introduction work? Does it start with a story? Can I find a thesis in the first paragraph(s)? If not, where *is* the thesis, if the essay has one?
- Taking a bird's-eye view of the essay, what do I notice about its structure? Does it use headings? Is it segmented into sections?
- What is the writer's "voice" like?
- How do the paragraphs look? What choices has the writer made about their length? What are the transitions like between them?
- If I read just the first sentences of each paragraph consecutively, what do I notice about the essay's structure?
- How has the writer concluded? What connection does the last paragraph have to do with the first?
- Does the author do anything that I might like to try out myself?

EXERCISE 1
The Practice of Imitation

Imitation of a writer's style or craft is *not* a form of plagiarism. In the visual arts, aspiring artists are often taught to imitate a particular artist or work in order to develop skills that can strengthen their own style. You might have seen one of them sitting in front of a painting in a museum, making their own sketch of what they see; you might have been one of them yourself. Writers too can use imitation as a form of practice.

Try it: Imitate something about the way a writer you like writes. For example:

- Choose one of their sentences and incorporate its structure into in your writing.
- Write in a "voice" like theirs.
- In your own way, use a word or concept they have used.
- Describe the kinds of things they describe—moods, weather, streetscapes, the look of people, etc.
- Use a technique of theirs—headings with titles, say—in your own essay.

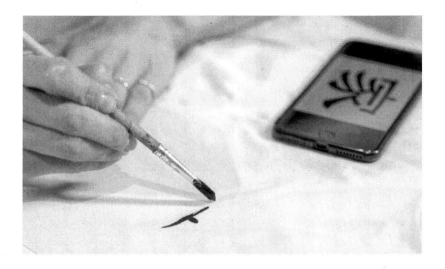

What Other Writers Can Give You: New Words

Some readers skip over words they don't know without even noticing. Instead, I urge you to see unfamiliar words as interesting offerings from fellow writers. Here's a standard way to work with words you don't know:

- *If you come upon a new word, note it.*
- *If you have seen or heard the word before,* especially multiple times, the chances are that you will see the word again. Look it up and consider trying it out in your own writing.
- *If you haven't heard the word before but can see that its meaning is important to understanding the text*—for example if the writer repeats it multiple times—look it up. You won't be able to understand the text without it.
- *If you haven't heard the word before and it doesn't seem necessary for understanding the text*, there's no pressing need to look it up. There are only so many new words you can hold in your head, and it might be an obscure word you won't see again.

What Other Writers Can Give You: Help Identifying Your Own Taste

Just as no two people like exactly the same foods, no two readers like exactly the same texts. What is your particular sensibility when it comes to reading?

What sorts of essays do you personally like, admire, and enjoy? What kinds of essays do *not* work for you?

Developing and understanding your own taste in essays will give you a clearer sense of the essays you most want to write. Try asking questions like these:

- As you read the essay, do you like the author? *What have they done in their essay* to make you feel that way?
- What in particular do you like and/or dislike about their voice?
- What is your opinion of the way they have structured their essay?
- What is their subject? Would you like to write on a similar one?
- What do you notice about the construction of their sentences?
- If they refer to other texts, how do they do it?

MAIN ASSIGNMENT

Once You Have a Workable Draft, Get Feedback from Others, and Then Write Your Final Revision

WORK WITH PEERS

For guidance on getting feedback from others, or working in peer groups, consult Part 5 of this book. For this assignment, let your peers know your concerns about your draft before they read it. You might ask in particular about the following, along with any other questions you have:

- Is my thesis clear to you? In your opinion, what is it?
- How do you think my examples from the text help you understand my thesis?
- In your view, should I make any adjustments in the way I have introduced and presented evidence?
- What do you notice about my introduction and conclusion—is it clear how I get from one to the other?
- Where in the essay do you feel most engaged, and why? Where do you lose interest?
- What is your response to my thesis?

FINISH YOUR ESSAY ON A TEXT

As you move toward finalizing your revision, read your essay aloud with your readers in mind. Here are some questions to consider one last time:

- Have you addressed the assignment properly?
- Does your overall organization, and your move from one idea to the next, make good sense as a way of proving your thesis? When you read just your introduction and then your conclusion, can you appreciate the way the essay develops?
- Are your quotes and references to the text sufficient evidence for your thesis? Are they cited correctly?
- Is your voice consistent?

When your answer is "yes" to these questions, you have finished your essay. Congratulations!

Writing a Research Essay

8

Confront Your Research Assignment

EXERCISE 1

Have you written a research paper before? What was its topic and what do you remember about your process? How did it turn out? What topics would you like to learn more about through research?

Research essays might seem to you to be the opposite of personal writing, since they depend on your engagement with something outside yourself. However, "your personal experience" and "something outside yourself" are not entirely separate things! You certainly might look outward when writing a personal essay, and an essay researching something unrelated to your life may well include varying degrees of your personal experience, whether visible to the reader or not.

In any case, the research essay is an outward-looking form that can be invigorating for writers, and also exciting and fun. There are many types of

research essays, of course, which vary greatly by academic field. But what they have in common is that they contain material that the writer has gathered through the library—books, essays, documents, etc.—or through methods like surveys, interviews, experiments, and so forth. *Readers of research essays expect* you to present whatever you discover in your research in a systematic, clear way that comes together around an argument or idea.

For some reason, the word "research paper" can fill some students with dread. Why do so many expect to be bored or miserable when they get a research paper assignment?

I think it's because they can see *personal* essays as the "fun" stuff, and *research* essays as nothing but "work." As you now know, though, crafting a good personal essay involves quite a bit of "work": revising, doubting yourself, and dealing with obstacles as you strive to make your essay a coherent and engaging whole. But yes, that work also provides many "fun" rewards, if by fun we mean freely expressing your own quirky self.

Research essays are "work," sure, but they too can be "fun." It's never either/or! Even if you're researching a subject you don't at first think will ever fascinate you, there are ways to put your own spin on it so your research engages you and becomes a statement of your thinking. Why settle for "phoning in" a research essay when you can go the route of being challenged as you explore an interesting subject?

Phoning in a research essay means skimming the surface of your topic, cobbling together random bits of research materials that don't necessarily connect well to each other or mean much to you. It means being bored while writing that essay, and that your professor will probably be bored while reading it.

Before I offer alternative directions, I want to take a few moments to look at what can get in the way of writing a research paper that only you can write.

Resistances

Here are some resistances to research writing. I'll offer you a *nudge* away from each one.

Not Understanding the Assignment

A surprising number of students begin research essays without fully understanding their assignment. They might be uncomfortable about asking for clarification, afraid that their fellow students, or the professor, will consider them unsophisticated or worse.

Nudge: The ability to ask questions and request clarification is a sign of a *good thinker*. If you have a question, the chances are that some—or even all!—of your classmates have the same one. Don't hesitate to take the risk of asking about any element of an assignment you don't understand, either by speaking out in class or in a private conversation with the professor.

Sometimes professors assume you understand what they mean when they use certain terms, like "analysis" and "argument," while in fact there is no single definition of those words that applies to all assignments. Depending on their academic discipline and their assignment's goal, your professors might define those words in a particular way. If you aren't sure, it's important to ask for clarification.

In general, an analysis is the process of examining all the parts of something, answering the question of "what" it's all about. Biologists analyze the digestive system to understand how it works; political scientists analyze data to see what issues voters are most concerned about.

An argument puts forth a perspective on or conclusion about the topic. That might mean answering the question of "why." "Why does the digestive system sometimes work poorly?" might lead to an argument like, "Proper nutrition can solve certain abdominal problems without medication"; the question, "Why are voters concerned about inflation?" might lead to an argument about how political ads work.

Research essays often require both analysis and argument.

Concern That Your Idea Is Superficial or Obvious

As you do research, you might get the feeling that others have covered your topic very well, leaving nothing new you could possibly come up with to say about it.

Nudge: Virtually no one researching something for the first time will have, or discover, a truly original idea about it right off the bat. An "obvious" idea, in fact, is a great place to start as you develop your thinking about any subject. Instead of letting the worry about being too obvious stop you in your tracks, keep in mind that starting with the obvious, and then exploring your genuine reactions and questions from there will help you craft a research essay that interests both you and others.

A "Lazy" Reluctance to Moving Beyond Your First Thoughts

Plenty of students are labeled by teachers, or by themselves, as "lazy." Research essays, perhaps because you are supposed to do them over an extended period of time, tend to bring out the "laziness" in many students. When they're given, say, two or three weeks to do a research project they might think, "Great—lots of time!" but then push it to the back burner as the days keep going by. Once they haven't done enough research before it's time to write, they aren't sure how to catch up, which leads to frantic struggles at the last minute to get pieces of research together too fast. "I am so lazy," they might say, "I just didn't spend enough time."

Maybe you too have felt "lazy" when faced with an assignment, perhaps simply not wanting to do the job at all. That could make you procrastinate, and otherwise make life difficult for yourself. But is it in fact laziness? What looks like laziness can be the result of many practical and psychological factors.

Nudge: If you're feeling lazy, be as honest as you can about what's going on. Maybe your "laziness" means that you're *stuck* somewhere in the process. What specifically were you doing in your writing/research when you decided you wanted to stop working? Perhaps something specific was in your way, like feeling daunted by a particular resource or resistance to your topic in general. Figuring that out, perhaps by getting help from a professor or peer can help you change something about whatever is difficult. Or maybe you just need a break—sometimes laziness is a reaction to being overwhelmed with too much to do. Can you find something fun to do for a limited time, and then come back?

Another way to resist laziness is to divide the task into very small steps. Can you make a plan to read one page of an article? That's a step. Do a freewrite about it? That's another. Create a list of as many baby steps as you like; checking them off will give you a feeling of satisfaction that can help you to do more.

Boredom with Your Topic in General

Sometimes a topic you're assigned can seem boring because you don't know anything about it and simply can't figure out how to find a way into it that sparks your interest. Or, on the other extreme, maybe you know many things

about the topic already and don't want to learn any more.

Nudge: An obvious solution is to talk with your instructor. They might help you find a particular angle on the topic that suits your purposes more readily. Or maybe they'll allow you to switch topics altogether.

If that doesn't work, try making a study of your own boredom. What exactly is it about the topic that bores you? If you don't have the option to switch topics, see if you can find a new angle. Let's say you're writing on a historical event and you're bored with stories about political maneuvers. The academic world welcomes a range of perspectives—could you look instead, perhaps, at the lives of women and families at home during the period, or gender dynamics in general, or the science of the bridges or weapons used in the events at hand, or the kind of popular culture the people were consuming? How about the sounds they were listening to?

An Aside: Sound Studies

The relatively new field of **sound studies** explores the sounds people hear, or heard, in a past or present social context. What sounds do you hear right now, and how do they affect your reading of this text? What sounds might people have heard in a historical period you have to write on? If that question happens to suit your interest, ask a librarian for help.

I don't know what you happen to find interesting, and unless they know you very well, neither does your professor. Only you can figure out what does not bore you. Cultivate *that*. Don't blame the topic for boring you—ask for help. Your professor, and/or a librarian, can help you find a focus on an inquiry that suits you. Keeping a targeted **Journal of Questions** (see below) could also help you discover your own angle of interest. You can find that angle if you put your mind to it.

Resistance to the Strictness of an Assigned Research Question

Maybe your instructor prefers that you do *not* find a new angle. Working with a specific question might be necessary to your learning in the class.

Nudge: You can still find a way to have a productive experience with your research paper. Get in touch with why it is in your interest to write about the topic, maybe through some private freewriting on topics like, "Why don't I like this topic?" and "What will I gain by working with it?" Maybe the answer is that you're looking for a good grade—that's a viable motive. Or maybe you appreciate that knowing about the seemingly "boring topic" will be useful to your education. Maybe you can discover a personal connection to the topic, perhaps via something in it that connects to something you already know? Is there any element of the topic that intrigues you more than others? Discussing such questions with someone else, or just with yourself, can help you become more engaged with your assignment.

Find or Refine Your Topic with a Journal of Questions

I will lead you through writing a research paper *on a topic of your choice.* Your professor, or future professors, might instead assign a specific question for research. You can adapt the following steps to that assignment too—I'll give you some tips about that as we go.

To find and clarify your topic, begin with a Journal of Questions, a version of the Journal of Noticings we did earlier.

Right now, off the top of your head, start reflecting on any potential subject you are curious about. For example, here's a list of questions that come to mind for me: What are the various uses of lavender as a scent? How do the practices of Islam work? What's going on with a certain congressional race in the American state of Ohio? What has happened in Hong Kong's recent history? What can I learn about South African dance music? What can I learn about neon lights?

What's *your* list? Start one today and, for at least a few days, continue to add items to it in your Journal of Questions. If you have an assigned topic, you can list questions *only about that topic.*

When you have a robust list, take some time to reflect on it, perhaps with a friend. Choose an item on it that seems the most interesting, challenging, and fun to research.

Decide on Your First Research Question

It's hard to find something if you don't know what you're looking for. In research, it helps to have a pointed question to guide your research.

Let's imagine that your chosen topic is, "What can I learn about neon lights?" The next step is to become at least a bit more specific. Invite your friends and classmates to pitch questions that could help you draw out a question that gets at what interests you most. For example, you could think as a scientist: "What is neon and where does it come from? How is it shaped into useable lights?" Or as an artist: "How do designers use neon to change indoor and outdoor space? Are different colors of neon useful for different kinds of effects?" Or a psychologist, "What effects do neon lights have on people?"

You might write a question for multiple items on your list—"How and where did lavender develop as a preferred scent in soaps?" "What are the main components of Islamic beliefs and practices?" before committing to one.

Don't worry just yet about how your questions will move toward an essay—your chosen question will probably evolve once you start doing research—that's part of the process.

Incidentally, if the topic of your research paper is not up to you, the chances are that you won't be given a general topic, like "slavery in the British Caribbean" or "Critics' views of Hemingway." Your assignment will probably be in the form of a research question. "Why did slavery end in the British Caribbean in 1833–34?" or "How have gender theorists critiqued Hemingway's novels?" Like all good research questions, these have multiple, debatable answers. Make sure you understand what sort of research your assignment requires. If your assignment provides you a with a concrete question, you can skip to the next section.

The specific question you settle on should invite multiple interpretations. "Was Hemingway interested in male characters?" doesn't work very well, since the answer is a simple "yes." But "How do gender theorists approach Hemingway?" could work well.

Here are some pitfalls to avoid as you arrive at your question:

- *It shouldn't have one answer you could easily look up*: "What is the brightest star in the Big Dipper constellation?" isn't a useful research question, but "What do astronomers know about the different stars in the Big Dipper?" could be a good place to start.
- *It shouldn't be so broad that you can't possibly cover it*: A topic like, "What is the history of psychiatric drugs?" probably wouldn't work unless you're writing a book. You could narrow it down, though, by choosing a specific drug, condition, or time period.
- *It shouldn't be too obvious*: "Is it important for parents to love their children?" The answer is "yes," but it doesn't take you anywhere. However, "What is the effect on children of not being loved?" might work.

- *It shouldn't be unanswerable*: "Why do bad things happen to good people?" It's a question we all might have, but is there any answer? However, something like, "How does the death of a beloved peer affect teenagers?" may move you in a workable direction.
- *It shouldn't be too vague*: "What do dreams mean?" However, "how did Freud view dreams?" could be a good start.

Depending on your topic, it can be useful to include a **hypothesis** in your research question: "Why did slavery end in the British Caribbean in 1833–34?" is wide open to anything you find. But a working hypothesis you could embed in your question, such as, "Did the enslaved peoples themselves have a role in ending slavery in the British Caribbean in 1833–34?" would put a particular spin on your search for sources.

Read Research Essays As You Prepare to Write One

As you decide on your research question it can be very useful to read some published research essays, whether they are directly connected to your topic or not. Read them as a writer, asking questions about how they work. For example:

- What is the author's research question?
- How does it appear in the essay? (Is it explicit in the introduction? Is it implied? Does it evolve in the course of the essay?)
- How does the author organize the essay as a whole? (Headings? Figures? Types of examples?)
- What research materials are part of the essay?
- How does the author introduce and discuss them?
- What does the conclusion look like?
- How does the writer cite the sources?

If you see strategies you like or appreciate, consider making use of variations on them in your own essay.

MAIN ASSIGNMENT

Decide on Your Research Question

Decide on a research question that fascinates you. You might try it out on classmates, friends, and your professor, with a goal of pointing it toward whatever interests you most in your topic. The more interested you are as a writer, the likelier you will be to engage your readers as well.

9

Do Your Research

EXERCISE 1
Preliminary Step

Once you have a research question, it's a good idea to organize yourself with a freewrite: What do you now know about the topic and what do you want to know?

If your assignment allows you to include personal material in your essay, your freewrite might include material that could become part of your draft—for example, your own reasons for wanting to research your topic. "I am going to South Africa, and want to learn about their dance scenes before I go." You could also include your preconceptions about the topic, which may or may not change or evolve as you do your research. "I saw so much neon when I went to Times Square in New York City, and I want to learn how it works."

But even if material in this freewrite has no place in your eventual essay, it is a useful way to lay out your interests, doubts, and

expectations before you begin your draft. And it can be your guide for doing something that quite a few students are oddly reluctant to do, much to the consternation of faculty: consult a librarian!

Finding Sources

On Your Own

Like many students, you might begin your search by consulting Google, Wikipedia, or YouTube. Such sources can be very useful, but it is crucial that you approach them with a scholar's eye. Most importantly, that means you are aware of where the information you find comes from.

Google can lead you to many viable and legitimate sites, like respected newspapers and many others, but if you find a source you don't know, make sure to figure out who sponsors it, and what their expertise is. Does their information check out anywhere else?

For example, let's say you discover a site that tells you that people have contacted visitors from outer space. Did it really happen? Check newspapers first—if they don't say anything about the story, it probably hasn't happened! But could it be a secret? Well, check the legitimacy of the sponsors of the website you're looking at. Do they have scientific degrees, publications, or other recognizable credentials? Are there other places where their information can be checked out? If not, you're probably not looking at a truthful website.

In doing academic research, **truthful information is essential**. All fields of academic thought are devoted to exploring and learning about the world as it is. Academics constantly add to each other's work; as they know more, they move even closer to the truth. When they find mistakes or untruths, they strive to correct them.

An Aside: Crowd-Sourcing

Crowd-sourcing is a method in which a request for information is sent to a group of people, often online. For example, "I'm going to ask all my friends on social media what I should do about my hair."

Crowd-sourcing legitimacy varies greatly. Your friends on social media may or may not know what they are talking about, but Wikipedia, which crowd-sources its information by allowing readers to edit and post, has constraints for the many volunteers who monitor its material. It can be a good start for research when you assess its information by comparing it to other sources and checking references.

Verification of information is important. You can trust academic articles from your database, but you should verify sources from places like YouTube (has a video been manipulated? Find out!), and other online sources. Some professors forbid you from using sources like Wikipedia, but others will allow it. Always ask your professor or librarian if you have a question about a source's legitimacy.

For more information about vetting online sources, my college's librarian told me about a very useful open-access (free), downloadable book called *Web Literacy for Student Fact-Checkers*. Google it!

With a Librarian

Your college or university library most likely houses impressive digital and print material that will take you a very long way from whatever you might find on Google. Some professors might ask that you consult "peer-reviewed articles," which are articles in academic journals vetted by peers who are also experts in their field. You'll find those in the many academic databases your library probably subscribes to, such as JSTOR, a database of academic journal articles, which also contains some primary-source documents; Artstor, for images; the American Library of Congress; the "19th-Century British Pamphlets" collection; the Congressional Record, for American politics; newspapers from all over the world, and on and on.

The best way to navigate among all these sources is to work with a librarian.

Every college or university library has at least one librarian on staff whose job is to help you figure out how to approach your topic and find useful sources.

Academic librarians are well trained in how to approach *any* topic. (Many specialize in a particular arena of research, but that specialization will only be relevant much later in your academic career when your research is more advanced—at this point, any librarian can help with your project).

Your librarian might also point you in the direction of sources outside the library—to more specialized libraries for example, some of which you can access online, or your school's student newspaper or other archives. Interviewing a professor, or someone else, who specializes in a particular topic might count, in some assignments, as a valid source, as might interviewing a range of classmates or others. Depending on your topic, open your mind to the many possibilities for sources you might not at first have considered as options.

"Primary" vs. "Secondary" Sources

Historians refer to "primary" sources as those that provide direct evidence of a historical event, such as newspaper articles, public records, letters, invoices, and other documents or artifacts. In contrast, "secondary" sources are those based on someone else's conclusions, such as articles written by other historians. In literature, a primary source is the studied authors' writings; secondary sources are essays scholars have written about those writings.

While Consulting Sources

Use Writing

If you use strategic freewriting as an integral and necessary part of your research, constructing your draft will be far easier than it would be if you simply read the sources and put them aside days before beginning your essay.

Immediately after you read an article, watch a video, consult a government document, or engage with any source—or even partway through the process of consulting it—pause and give yourself five minutes or so just to freewrite. Here are some questions to consider, with no planning in advance:

- What did you learn from the source?
- What interested you most? Did you have other personal reactions? Excited? Uncomfortable? Confused? Satisfied? Curious?
- What idea or question does your source raise that speaks to your research question?
- What sections of it are most noteworthy for you? Why?
- How have your ideas about your paper changed or evolved after consulting this source?

You don't have to write on all of these, and don't worry if your answers blur together as you freewrite. The point is to dig into your reactions now to help you write your draft later.

Freewriting about sources is an easy way for you to record what you learn from your research. Incorporate direct quotes from your sources (noting where they came from so the information is handy later). You might even end up generating passages you can place directly into your essay's draft.

Don't worry too much about your essay's structure when you're in this researching/freewriting process. However, if something occurs to you about a sequence of ideas that might work well in your essay, write it down!

Be Open to Tweaking Your Research Question

There's nothing wrong with making changes in your research question once you are doing research. In fact, it can be a sign that your research is working well. Your very first source could lead you to a question you find richer, even if it's more specific, than your original one. "What role did enslaved peoples have in ending slavery in the British Caribbean in 1833–34," for example, might lead you to the Haitian slave rebellion, which you might find to be an intriguing topic in itself. "What allowed the slave rebellion in Haiti to happen?" might become your new research question. Of course, if your new question moves too far away from your professor's assigned question, consult with the professor about any switch.

Alternatively, if your research question leads you to dead ends that don't interest you, you could shift gears. "What do critics say about Hemingway?" might lead you to a swamp of articles that you have trouble wading through. But you might then find an article on Hemingway's relationship to his maleness that opens a different research question, maybe along the lines of: "How did Hemingway's public image as a macho writer affect his personal life?"

EXERCISE 2
Report on Your Research

It can be useful to write an informal research report to a classmate, your teacher, or the whole class after you have done some research:

- What sources have you consulted and how has your research question evolved?
- Do you think you have enough material for your essay, or do you plan to consult more sources? Which ones?
- Is there a difficulty you're concerned about as you move toward writing your essay?
- What ideas do you have about how your essay might proceed?

MAIN ASSIGNMENT

Your Research Work

Starting from your research question, begin researching your topic. Form the building blocks of your essay by writing freewrites on your findings as you go. Make periodic reports to your classmates, friends, and/or professor, either in writing or simply by talking, about how your work is going. Sharing and discussing your process will help you manage it.

10

Write Your Research Essay

Turn Your Research Question into a Statement

Read through all your freewrites with your research question in mind and find a way to turn that question into a statement, based on what you have discovered.

For example, the question, "How did Hemingway's public image as a macho writer affect his personal life?" could become, "While Hemingway's public image was that of a macho writer, in his private life he was filled with mixed feelings about his male and female sides."

That sentence might not yet become the essay's final argument, but it can serve as a guide for your essay's preliminary structure. For example, the first part of the essay on Hemingway could give examples of his public image, and the second could give examples, based on photographs and letters, of his private life.

Can You Use "I" in a Research Essay?

Some students assume that using the first person, "I," is always forbidden in research writing. That's often not the case. Ask your professor—some may prefer that you avoid "I," in the name of being as objective as possible. But probably most will be quite open to it. They will want you to let the reader know something of who you are as a researcher.

Of course, if you don't use "I," you are still using your personal insights and experience. Remember that you are writing an essay that only you can write!

Using "I" in most research essays does not mean telling personal stories. Your use of the first person might be to engage the reader more directly in your process of thinking, perhaps along the lines of, "I assumed X at first, but further research reveals Y, which allowed me to understand that Z ..."

However, your professor might invite you to write a "personal" research paper, in which you *do* include direct stories: "I chose to research Islam because I wanted to understand my Muslim friends better," say, or, "I was frustrated when I began researching neon, because many of the articles were too advanced for me. However, I discovered how it is used in art, and ...”

Begin to Structure Your Essay

When you feel you have enough material from your research to begin writing, it is time for your critical muscle to flex. Read through your notes and freewrites, marking sections you can potentially use in your essay.

From there, begin to think of how to order the sections you marked and how to structure your draft.

Are you ready to make a working outline of your essay?

If not, keep freewriting from your sources to gather more material, and look for more sources if you don't have enough. One way to know that you have enough material is if you can "answer" your research question. Begin by making an **informal list** of ideas you've found that provide answers. Then sketch out a **rough outline** that orders your ideas in a clear way. Here are two general ways to set up your outline.

Choose a Deductive or Inductive Argument Structure

Most research essays are written **deductively**, in the form of a thesis-and-proof structure. In your first paragraph or two, you present your thesis, a "statement that answers your research question." From there, you present the evidence from your research to back it up, using multiple paragraphs in an order that works for your purpose. For example, here are some potential sequences of examples:

- From less significant to most significant
- From earlier in time to later in time
- From one geographical location to another
- From analysis—laying out the components of your subject, answering the "what" question—to argument, asserting your point of view on the "why" or "how" (see Chapter 8)
- Or in another order that fits with your topic.

You could also use the same general order of evidence, but not let the reader in on your thesis until the end. That's called writing **inductively**—it poses the problem or question at the beginning, then presents evidence in steps that lead the reader through various steps toward the thesis, which is only stated at the end.

Once you have an overall structure in mind, it is useful to write a rough, annotated outline that organizes the information you want to present. You might remember that in Chapter 2 we discussed making a "rough outline" of a personal essay, after gathering freewrites and other materials. When writing a research paper, it can be useful to write a similar rough outline, annotated by the evidence you've gathered in research.

For example, here's an annotated outline by a historian building an inductive essay on the research question, "What caused enslaved peoples in the British Caribbean to be freed in 1833–34?" The following annotated outline begins with the question, and then is organized chronologically through answers given by various theorists; we don't know the author's answer to the research question—the thesis—until the last paragraph:

- **Introduction, Raising the Research Question**: *Why did Great Britain, by far the largest enslaving nation in the 1700s, end its slave trade, and slavery in 1833–34?* Briefly introduce the point that historians have differed greatly about this over the years.

- **Paragraph or Section**: *An early theory*, popularized by nineteenth- and early twentieth-century liberal British historians, points to the humanitarian movement of evangelicals in Britain who applied their non-conformist ethical religious views to their humanitarian concern about the abuse of enslaved Africans and Creoles.

- **Paragraph or Section**: *However, by the mid-twentieth century new generations of historians began to question this self-congratulatory interpretation.* A prominent example was Eric Williams, an African Trinidadian historian who argued in 1944 that the freeing was not due to humanitarian concerns, but to the early development of industrial capitalism in Britain. British elites, said Williams, concluded that free wage labor was cheaper than slave labor.

- **Paragraph or Section**: *Later, other historians began to argue that Williams's view was too narrowly focused on economic factors.* They saw the rising campaign for abolition in early nineteenth-century Britain as the result of the emergence of an urban middle-class political movement seeking to democratize British politics by introducing various reforms.

● **Paragraph or Section**: Finally, influenced largely by both 1950s–60s African American civil rights movements and global movements for the independence of British colonies in Africa and the Caribbean, *other historians began researching the role of enslaved peoples themselves.* They noted that enslavers in the British Caribbean and England had become fearful of slave rebellions in the aftermath of the Haitian Revolution of 1791–1804, and eventually concluded that British elites finally accepted ending slavery in 1833 to preserve their sugar colonies and not lose them the way France did in Haiti in 1804.

● **Conclusion and Thesis**: *Enslaved peoples themselves were responsible for their own freedom. It's striking how little attention white historians paid for over a hundred years to the actual experiences and thoughts of enslaved peoples*, especially in how their actions in the Caribbean influenced colonial politics in Britain itself. More work is needed to uncover sources revealing the thinking and behavior of enslaved peoples in the Caribbean and elsewhere in the Americas.

EXERCISE 1
Write an Annotated Rough Outline

Write an informal, annotated, rough outline of your essay for your teacher and classmates. Include your thesis (the answer to your research question) either at the beginning of your essay (for a deductive argument), or at the end after you've led the reader to it (for an inductive argument).

Separating Sections of Your Essay

I referred to each stage in the outline above as a "paragraph or section." Students sometimes wrongly get the idea that each element in an argument should have a single, sometimes overly long, paragraph. There's no reason for that; if you like, feel free to take a few paragraphs to present any piece of evidence.

Headings: You might consider organizing your research essay by dividing it into separate sections, each with either a numbered heading or a title. Essays sometimes come to life when you break up the narrative by leading the reader through various stages, and headings can make the organization clearer not only to you the writer, but to your readers as well. The titles of your headings can help orient the reader to what you are saying in a particular section. For example, notice how headings work in this book—they divide sections by theme.

Your Introduction

As with all forms of essays, it can be most useful to write your introduction only after you have developed the rest of your essay. When you're ready, here are a few options for introducing a research essay:

Begin with a general discussion of the issue before stating your thesis. Here's an example: "For much of the twentieth century, Hemingway was viewed as the epitome of masculinity. His hunting, fishing, and womanizing gave him the image of a rugged man's-man. However, recent critics have been hinting at the idea that in fact he had a far more complicated relationship with his gender identity than most people realized. We now have evidence of the truth of those hints."

Begin with a story appropriate to your topic, perhaps one you choose from your research. For example, the story of Hemingway's mother dressing him as a girl when he was a child would prepare the reader for a research essay about Hemingway's fluid gender identity.

Use your introduction to compare two perspectives on your question, ending with your thesis. For example: "There are many debates about the drinking age in various countries. In the United States, the legal age of twenty-one is especially high. Some say this protects young people from the dangers of drinking, and especially of driving while drunk. However, others believe that the higher drinking age makes the problem worse by causing teenagers to over-drink in private and then drive. As I will show, evidence points to the validity of the latter view, which leads me to argue that the drinking age in the United States is too high."

STUDENT EXAMPLE
An Introduction to a Research Essay on Hurricanes in The Bahamas

Here is a student's epigraph (opening quote) and three-paragraph introduction to a research paper on how climate change causes increasingly intense hurricanes, which eventually concludes with a list of what people can do to help improve the situation.

From this introduction, the student went on to explain what she had learned in her research about climate change's effect on The Bahamas. The second part of her essay was on worldwide efforts to solve the problem.

"Had first video conference with my youngest daughter today. Showed her the most beautiful place from space. #Bahamas."

In the summer of 2015, NASA astronaut Scott Kelly sent this tweet out to the world. Pristine ice-blue waters, beautiful beaches, and sandbars giving the country light strokes of watercolors from a bird's-eye view made his statement true.

Four years later, on September 1, 2019, Hurricane Dorian made landfall on the Abaco islands before continuing on to the island of Grand Bahama the following day. At the time I had just made it to New Jersey for my senior year of high school with the company of my mother who was there to help me move into the dorm while my dad and brother were back in our home in Nassau, The Bahamas praying for the best. Luckily for them, Dorian remained offshore as it passed Nassau, and heavy rains and flooding were the extents of the damage. Landing in the Abacos as a category 5 hurricane, however, Hurricane Dorian became the strongest tropical cyclone to ever affect The Bahamas, with sustained wind speeds of 185 mph (Sant & Bowman 2019).

For some odd reason, climate change has become this big, all-encompassing debate that the whole world can't seem to get behind. That's the issue right there, that the whole world can't get behind it. It's not that so much damage has been done that it's impossible to reverse, it's that without a confident consensus that it is without a doubt happening, climate change becomes impossible to reverse. How can we solve a worldwide problem that half the population is turning a blind eye to? We can't. (OM)

Your Conclusion: Two Options

Point back to your introduction. Before you write the conclusion to your research paper, make sure to reread your introduction. Where has your essay led you from there? Is there some idea or image from your introduction that you could pick up on in the conclusion? Doing so will give satisfying closure to your essay.

Summarize briefly as part of your conclusion. It is usually a good idea to include at least a brief overview of your answer to your research question. "Given the evidence, it's very clear that Hemingway's macho image was a careful construction. While it was based on his own self-image as a manly man, an examination of his private activities and preoccupations has revealed that it was textured and complex, and that 'femininity' was an important component of his identity."

Point to the future. Researching a topic often uncovers further topics that you'd like to see more research on. Your conclusion is a good way to share those topics, as we saw in the "more work is needed to uncover sources revealing the thinking and behavior of enslaved peoples" remark in the conclusion of the example above. Another example: "This is the beginning of an understanding of Hemingway's complexity when it comes to gender. I hope that literary critics continue to question not only *his* gender identity, but that of woman writers and public figures who have been assumed to be solely 'womanly.'"

You might acknowledge the other side of your argument in your conclusion, if only to explain how you find it to be wrong. "I have demonstrated that twenty-one years old is far too old for one's first drink, and in fact, most Americans have had plenty of drinks when they reach that age. Why not make it legal? As I have shown, I am very sympathetic to the efforts of those who strive to avoid lethal car accidents, but I am also convinced that a higher drinking age is not the way to prevent them."

STUDENT EXAMPLE
Conclusion on Climate Change and Hurricanes in The Bahamas

Warm oceans don't just help storms get going, they increase the storm surge as well. When freshwater ice sheets melt in the ocean, "it contributes a greater volume of meltwater than it originally displaced" (Noerdlinger). My research has shown that "a rapid disintegration of Antarctica's ice sheets could push sea level up much faster and higher, by as much as 4 to 10 feet by 2100" (Berwin) ... High sea levels in addition to a storm surge sets up a high hazard for devastating flooding, particularly in coastal communities (Rahmstorf 2017).

In a place like The Bahamas, there's no place for all of that flooding to go, so all that rain and seawater build up our pristine ice-blue waters like a bathtub with a drain clogged until your couch is floating in your living room. Benson Etienne, a 15-year-old boy living in Abaco at the time Dorian hit said, "We had to swim for our lives in dirty water, fighting against strong currents. Now everything is destroyed, every school. There is no water to drink" (Etienne 2019). The world needs to realize that everything is connected. Climate change might not have affected you yet, but it will eventually. The Bahamas felt it with Dorian, and

California is feeling it today with forest fires. You will never know when it's your turn to suffer until that day comes. That should be reason enough to realize that the time for change is now. (OM)

Fears May Arise When Writing a Research Essay

Writing a good research paper requires that you get into the habit of questioning your assumptions. That can be difficult, because you might not want to change your mind about issues you believe in. Not every topic will make you change once you dig into it, of course, but more often than you might think, serious research makes us question ideas we never thought we would question. And resistance to changing our minds can get in our way, for example by pushing us not to care much about what we write, because it can be safer not to care.

Of course, opening yourself up to changing your worldview through research and study, while potentially scary, is ultimately very exciting. In fact, its scariness can be the thing that *makes* it exciting. That might be obvious when it comes to personal essay writing, in which the scariness of self-exposure is right there in front of you. But it can happen, albeit differently, in research writing too when you take risks. Is exposing your *intellectual* quirks and questions a way of becoming "naked" in a way that might scare you?

STUDENT EXAMPLE
A First-Year Student's Writing about a Research Essay
on Originalism in Interpreting the US Constitution

I knew I wanted to talk about originalism because it has interested me for a long time. I definitely had some worries going into the assignment, however, because I felt like I was taking a risk talking about something where I didn't already have a position that I wanted to argue. This was the first time I wrote an essay without a pre-established argument that I was trying to defend. I hoped my research and reflection would result in a conclusion, and I was pleased that it did.

I started this assignment with the question of whether or not originalism is a valid method of interpreting the US Constitution. I was really curious and eager to learn more about the subject, so I started my research pretty early on. I began to rummage through the vast amount of scholarly articles, ebooks, and videos on originalism and was able to find a lot of great material that I could both use as evidence and as a way to expand my thinking ... But the more research I did, the more questions I felt that I had to answer along the way to assess whether originalism was the right way to interpret the Constitution. This initially worried me, because I thought that if I went down the path of answering more questions, those questions would lend themselves to even more questions, and I wouldn't ever have a coherent paper. This was luckily not the case ... I was able to consider other questions ... in a way that strengthened my thesis. (GK)

STUDENT EXAMPLE
A First-Year Student's Writing about a Research Essay on Whether Abortion Should Be Legal

Something that I'm really proud of in this essay was how easily it came to me to include my own opinions and stories ... If you are truly passionate and interested in the topic you're writing about, ideas will flow from you.

Initially, I thought I would write about the different perspectives on abortion, including the different perspectives from pro-life people but as I started writing, this whole idea about Separation of Church and State came through which led me to focus on those who identify as religious and pro-life ... This is an issue that I've always heard about, and one that is also extremely relevant now so it ... fueled my interest in the topic even further and taught me new things, such as how "backstreet abortions" happened.

Another consideration that I didn't initially think about was how the patriarchy impacts women's choice on abortion. I knew that I was against men making decisions for women but I didn't fully realize that what we're living in is patriarchy, so doing research on that helped. Also learning about why women still believe in this patriarchy put into perspective why there are still women today who support the patriarchy and led me to understand my own family a little bit more.

... This was the most fun-to-write research paper because in the past, I've always had to remain objective or side with one side (argumentative), but even then I was never allowed to include my personal opinions; I was told to just go off the facts that I find. With this paper though, I was able to not only include my own opinions, but also my own story. This made the paper so much more personal to me which just makes writing more interesting and fun. (EO)

As you construct your essay, note fears, frustrations, and other emotions in personal freewrites. They may be entirely private, or maybe they will give you material you can use in your essay.

Keep going, remembering that you're writing a draft you can polish later.

MAIN ASSIGNMENT

Draft Your Research Essay

At this point you should have plenty of writings to go on, but they might seem haphazard and unorganized. You might begin by taking a bird's eye view of your essay—whether or not your research question has evolved, make it into a statement of your overall thesis or plan. From there, find a tentative structure of your essay, and construct a rough, annotated outline of where you want to go. Start writing the pieces of your essay, maybe beginning with what you have to say about your evidence, or else your introduction and conclusion. It can be useful to write the parts you are more confident about first, and move from there, as opposed to developing the draft in the order it will ultimately be in. Trust your instincts!

Get Feedback on Your Draft and Revise It

MAIN ASSIGNMENT

Finish Your Essay

When you have a complete draft, get feedback from peers and others.

Then revise your essay, making it exactly the way you want it. Read it aloud, to yourself or to anyone who will listen, and do some final tweaks.

Make sure to add a Works Cited list that follows the system your professor approves of. If you're not sure, ask your professor. You can find guides online about how to cite various sources in MLA, APA, or other citation formats.

Write a process letter to hand in with your final draft. It might include answers to the following questions:

- What in particular am I proud of when I read through my draft?
- What are some moments in my process of getting to this final version in which I struggled and/or learned something important?

- What do I notice about who I am as a writer as I reflect on the process of getting to this final essay?

Congratulations! You've finished your essay.

PART FOUR

Mindfulness and Essay Writing

12

Introductory Thoughts on Mindfulness

Maybe you're a person who almost never seeks a quiet moment to tune into your own mind. Or maybe you already meditate on a regular basis. Whatever your relationship is to mindfulness practices, they can enhance your work as an essay writer.

In particular, they can help you with three overall goals:

- To become more deeply aware of your own thoughts, thereby generating more ideas for writing
- To understand and tackle the way your thoughts and feelings get in your way when you are writing (or trying to write)
- To become more aware of what does and does not work for you as a writer in terms of the form and content of your essays

To help you achieve those goals, this part has two sections. In this chapter I introduce mindfulness and discuss the ways in which it may offer us calm or clarity. In Chapter 13 I address how it interacts with the psychology of

writing and offer practical suggestions about using mindfulness during your writing process.

My *Writing and Mindfulness* classes always begin with three to five minutes of meditation. I tell the students to "feel your body sitting in the seat," "scan your inner landscape," and "pay attention to your breath."

Some students eagerly focus right away on their inner selves. But others, especially at the beginning of the semester, squint open their eyes, peek at their classmates, and fidget. They seem to feel awkward in response to the direction to tune inward, in spite of the fact that they have signed up for a class with "mindfulness" in its title. Even after a week or two, when the pattern of opening meditation has set in as part of our class practice, a few students continue to be uncomfortable when the direction comes to just sit and be with themselves. Isn't it amazing how hard that can be?

As weeks go by, though, everyone comes around. Students look at me expectantly as I enter the room, waiting for me to gong my little bell. When it sounds, I no longer need to tell them it is time to close their eyes.

The practice of sitting quietly answers a need our bodies all have and often don't get enough of: time just to sit calmly with ourselves, with nothing at all to do.

Mindfulness and Our Bodies

I'm one of those people who does yoga and meditates. But until recently I kept that part of my life quite separate from my work as a college professor. Teaching academic writing, I figured, wasn't connected at all with what was going on in my students' bodies. It's all about thinking! But those two parts of my life kept bumping up against each other. For a long time I had said, in response to students telling me about various problems, "How about doing a private freewrite about what's bothering you?" In helping them get beyond procrastination, I had asked, "What happens exactly when you sit down to write?" Or "What has worked best for you when it comes to finishing an essay?"

Those private freewrites and inner self-explorations, I realized, were ways of using "mindfulness." Yes, they are cognitive activities: we do them with our minds. However, they also invite, and even require, that we consult our bodies too as we seek comfort or new ideas.

Laraine Herring, a professor who writes about mindfulness in writing, talks about "deep writing," the kind that "comes from our bodies, from our breath ... from dissolving our egos so that the real work can emerge through us ..." (7). That might sound a bit more dramatic than the work you do in your essays for college, but she makes an important point about where our "deepest"—most powerful and interesting—writing comes from. "It's easy for us to forget," she continues, "the importance of the body in the writing process. Indeed, language does come from the mind, but the stories that spring from the authentic voice that is ours and ours alone come from within our bodies ... Our bodies have stored all of our experiences. They are there, waiting for us" (7).

Mindfulness exercises enhance your writing by helping you gain better access to the experiences and ideas that are stored in your body, whether you've been aware of them before or not. Freewriting does that too, and I would call it one form of mindfulness.

Defining Mindfulness

What exactly *is* mindfulness? It's a common buzzword these days, used in a very wide range of contexts: mindful golf, mindful parenting, mindful eating, mindful—you name it, and someone probably thinks you can do it better if you're mindful.

In spite of the fact that it is often used to help us be more successful and accomplish practical things, the word "mindfulness" still retains a whiff of something you do *apart* from your regular life. That's probably because of its associations with the mindful traditions that exist in virtually all religions. In any mosque, temple, church, or other place for gatherings of spiritual people there are moments of silent contemplation or prayer, during which people's bodies are still as they turn their focus inward, or away from the material world. The popularity of secular mindfulness, I'd say, is an acknowledgement of the power of those quiet moments.

Outside of religious practices, our daily lives too often lack any time for quiet contemplation. If we happen on such a moment—waiting in line, say—we often pull out our phone for distraction. Young people are often criticized for doing that, but it's an issue across ages and cultures. I've seen plenty of older people—haven't you?—poking at their phones as they sit in waiting rooms or ride on trains, or even in the middle of a faculty meeting.

Nevertheless, and no matter how we may try to avoid it, our bodies can't help longing for the wonderful experience of just sitting and being, with nothing to do other than look around calmly, or tune into our inner selves.

I think that need is the reason why yoga classes and other such experiences are popular among people with busy lives—they "force" us to get away from distractions and just be with ourselves.

That brings me to the working definition of mindfulness that I'll be using here: the practice of turning one's attention, without judgment, to one's inner experience, and quietly paying attention to it. We sometimes do that while freewriting, absolutely, but in doing so we're also engaging our intellects. Mindful sitting, with eyes closed, is a rawer way to bump up against our inner selves.

EXERCISE 1
Try Some Mindfulness

Read through the following directions first, and then go for it.

- Choose a place with as few distractions as possible, maybe a place you like outdoors, at your desk, or anywhere else.
- Sit quietly.
- If you prefer to have other people with you that's fine, provided they too are willing to sit quietly without interrupting you.
- Turn off your phone or other distractions, though first, if you like, set a timer for at least one minute, and maybe five or more.
- Close your eyes and tune inward. Notice your breathing. Slow it down and notice how it moves in and out of your chest or belly. As you do so, you'll probably notice thoughts. Can you take one step away from them and simply observe without judgment whatever is entering your head? Then turn your attention back to your breathing.

That's it! There are endless variations, but these simple steps are the basic ones.

The "without judgment" part of observing your inner thoughts can be much harder than you might think. As soon as many people "tune inward," they are flooded with ideas like, "I can't believe I said X yesterday, it was so stupid!" or "I shouldn't be angry about Y," or "I'm a terrible writer." Such thoughts involve self-judgment and often some amount of self-blame. Other people might direct criticisms outward: "she looks awful in that sweater," "he was so wrong to say that," or "this activity is ridiculous. It can't possibly help my writing."

When such thoughts flood your head as you're trying to sit calmly, they might make you *more* agitated instead of achieving the sense of peaceful calm that mindfulness is supposedly meant to lead you to.

But that agitation is not a problem! It's part of the process, because the goal of mindfulness is not to change or get rid of your thoughts, but to strive to *accept* whatever is in your head. It is simply an invitation to step back and *notice what is going on in your mind*, even if you can only get maybe one inch away from your inner judgments.

For example, let's say you're thinking, "I'm a terrible writer." You might expect that a mindful approach would insist that you force yourself to get rid of that feeling. But no. Mindfulness simply invites you to say, inside your head, between you and yourself, "I'm noticing that I keep telling myself I'm a terrible writer." That's it!

It might not sound like much, but as we'll see there's a huge difference between, "I'm a terrible writer" and "I notice that I keep telling myself that I'm a terrible writer." Mindfulness can't wipe the slate clean of our self-judgments and stop them cold, but its power, which turns out to be a mighty force, is to help us confront where our minds *actually are*. That can be an important step on the route to getting our minds to stop being stuck and move someplace else.

Many people think mindfulness means making your mind completely calm and blank. Students in my class sometimes apologize early in the semester, saying, "I'm sorry; I just can't clear my head!" My answer to that is, "Are you kidding me? Neither can I!"

Yes, certain people, including those who have practiced meditation for years, might be adept at getting their minds into a place we could call "blank." But even for them, the challenge is to *know what to do* with their pulsating inner clutter, not get rid of it altogether.

Have you heard people say that their best ideas come to them while taking a shower, on a jog, cooking, or driving? "The idea just popped into my head!" they say. "I have no idea where it came from." Maybe it's happened to you—activities in which you can't do much else besides what you're doing in the moment have an interesting ability to relax your mind. They open you up to any ideas that might want to burst out from the mysterious part of you, the place where your creative muscle's ideas come from.

Let's look more specifically at how mindfulness can help your writing.

Internal Mindfulness

Have you ever had the experience of submitting an essay to a teacher with your eyes closed, metaphorically, because you don't have a clear sense of what you've written, or why your teacher would or wouldn't like it?

That non-mindful experience often results in an unsatisfying grade, though at times you might get lucky. But even if you get an A you might not be sure what clicked for the teacher, and the experience probably does not feed you all that much. Of course, maybe the grade itself is all the nourishment you need—in that case it will probably give you a fast-food kind of satisfaction, not as nourishing as you might wish it could be. It's hard to be proud of writing you don't remember shaping with full consciousness.

I encourage you to take mindful responsibility for what you write. That means taking time with it, reading it over, and revising. You won't be able to predict in advance what your professor or audience will think, of course, but that inner mindfulness will give you the satisfaction of creating something that you yourself value.

One way to cultivate your inner mindfulness is by freewriting about your writing process, asking yourself what happens as you write, and noting where you do and don't get stuck. That's easier for some people than it is for others—I always remember a student who looked at me, dumbfounded, when I asked his class, on the day they were handing in their first essays, to write about how they had written them.

"What do you mean?" the student asked. "*I wrote the paper!*" He couldn't imagine that there was anything else to say, because he was not in the habit of reflecting on his own actions.

Some people have no problem examining their own writing process after they have written an essay, but others struggle at first to get any distance from their own experience. The mindful practice of "writing about the process of writing" is a way to cultivate that inner distance, which allows you to adjust your approaches to writing so they serve you better.

If your inner belief is, "I am a bad writer," for example, there isn't much you can do about it other than going through life bashing your own writing. But if you step back to say, "I notice that I keep telling myself I'm a bad writer," you give yourself space to tell yourself something else!

External Awareness

In addition to making you aware of your inner experience, mindfulness invites you to be more awake to what's around you.

Let's try that right now.

Take a moment to feel yourself in your body in the space and time you're in right now. Look around: what do you see, hear, smell, feel? How do those external elements affect your experience of reading this?

Here's how being mindful of your *external* environment can support your writing:

- *On a practical level.* How do the spaces where you write affect your writing? Do you write better alone? With others? In the library? In bed? In a café? Outside? Can you rearrange your physical writing experiences so they are more to your liking?

- *At school.* The external-orientation side of mindfulness means listening well to the goals and methods presented in your classes. What is happening in your classes? What are your professors asking of you? Develop your capacity to engage, question, and ask for help.

- *In your relationship to the world as a writer and person.* Mindfulness invites you to cultivate a curious mindset about what is around you. You're in a building, or outside, and you're part of a neighborhood, town, city, state, province, country, continent. Mindfulness helps you be more aware of the characteristics of those places, from physical forms and designs to the social and cultural attitudes held by the people around you. Most subjects you'll study—literature, psychology, botany, history, architecture, physics, chemistry, sociology, music—in fact, *all* academic subjects, connect in a range of ways to physical spaces. And yet many people live in and walk through those spaces without fully seeing and taking responsibility for where they are. The practices of looking, and being, that mindfulness nurtures ask you to make a point of looking at nuances beyond the familiar and obvious. That can make you not only a better writer, but a more engaged person, student, thinker, and friend.

A Difficulty with Mindfulness: Resistance to "The Present Moment"

As babies, we have a lot of mindfulness and curiosity. We pay attention, reach out, and want to know more; whether it's crying, babbling, eating, or playing, we take our present-moment experience very seriously.

But life experiences distract us as we grow, and we might unwittingly learn to sabotage our own openness. As we become more complicated, our minds travel in many different directions, and it becomes harder for us to stay in the present moment. We want to look away from certain things; we get hurt; we get stuck in dreams, or nightmares, about the past and the future. Sometimes our distractions pull at us so much that they drown out

our capacity to think and create in the present moment, even when we really want to.

The mindfulness solution is always that we should strive to focus back in on the good old present moment. "Be here, be now, feel your body in the space of this moment."

But is that really the answer? It's not so easy to do, and besides, what exactly is so great about the present moment, anyway?

Good question! Essayist Phillip Lopate, in fact, jokes about it in "Against Joie de Vivre": "I have lived in the present from time to time," he tells us. "[A]nd I can tell you that it is much overrated. Occasionally, as a holiday from stroking one's memories or brooding about future worries, I grant you, it can be a nice change of pace. But to 'be here now,' hour after hour, would never work ... Besides, the present has a way of intruding whether you like it or not. Why should I go out of my way to meet it?" (725).

He is playing with us, of course, and yet he has a point. Being in the present moment can feel like too much work! Nevertheless, the calm goal of mindfulness is to help you be right here where you are, a surprisingly useful place to be.

We usually find people who are "present" to be more appealing. Why? Part of it is that they are reacting *with you* to whatever is going on. They are awake to shifts and changes, not stuck in ideas that have meaning only to themselves. They are fun because they focus not only on themselves, but also on whatever the people around them say or do. That's often because they simply feel comfortable with themselves, either because they were lucky to have been loved while growing up, or because they have worked hard to develop the kind of inner sense of grounding that mindfulness provides.

You might not associate that present quality with writing. But being present as a writer can help you to (1) have a clear sense of your audience, and (2) be awake to the present moment of your own process. That's a good place to be when you want to create something new.

> ### EXERCISE 2
> ## *Noticing People*
>
> Here's an observational experiment you can do: notice the people around you, and/or think about people you know: what is their apparent relationship to the present moment? Do some seem to be right there with you, while others are more likely to be distracted by other thoughts? How does that affect your interactions with them?

"Radio NST"

Thich Nhat Hanh, the Vietnamese Buddhist practitioner who brought theories of mindfulness to the West in many books and presentations, attributes our difficulties with being present to the fact that most of us have an "internal radio station" in our heads, which he calls, Radio NST (Non-Stop Thinking).

"Even when we're sitting still," he says, "with no external stimuli, an endless internal dialogue may be going on in our head. We're constantly consuming our thoughts. Cows, goats, and buffalo chew their food, swallow it, then regurgitate and re-chew it multiple times. We may not be cows or buffalo, but we ruminate just the same on our thoughts— unfortunately, primarily negative thoughts. We eat them, and then we bring them up to chew again and again ... We need to learn to turn off Radio NST. It's not good for our health to consume from our own consciousness this way ..." (47–48).

Radio NST can get in the way of writing. Regurgitated thoughts and worries can fill you up so much that it's hard to get to the fresh, new, interesting writing that you have the capacity to produce.

The tool of mindfulness has a lot of potential to help you be present with your writing by taking responsibility for your inner Radio NST.

For example, can you close your eyes and watch your thoughts as a compassionate, uninvolved witness?

That's a genuine question, and I like phrasing it that way. *Can you?* I learned to say that from the language of yoga teachers, who use it a lot: Can you lift your arms up? Can you breathe into your belly? Can you watch your thoughts go by without grasping onto them?

Asking "can you" opens up to the possibility that the answer might be, "no, I can't." And that too is okay—in fact, it can be wonderful to acknowledge it if it's simply where you actually are. There's no need to pretend you can do something you can't.

Can you, or can you not? Either one is worth reflecting on. Any answer to "can you?" leads you to be in closer touch with the present moment and to being able to use that place—"I'm able to become fully present," or "I'm not able to"—as grounding in *reality*, which will help you see where you want to go next.

If you can't be present, you might feel stuck, including with your writing. Perhaps your mind is distracted from clarity because it's flitting around like a dragonfly, not entirely sure where it is or where it wants to go or land. With mindfulness, your only job is to notice that, and maybe just sit with your feeling.

When you *can* be fully present, including being present in the reality of your inability to be present, there's a paradox: the more you accept wherever you are, the easier it is for you to move somewhere else.

So when you think that mindfulness isn't possible, you can get closer to it by *accepting* the fact that it seems impossible. Accept that your writing doesn't seem to be working at all, get up, walk around, and it might look different when you get back. In contrast, if you're in an *unexamined* state of distractedness, you're more likely to be stuck in a truer sense, never able to escape from the annoying sounds of Radio Non-Stop Thinking pumping in your head.

The Psychology of Writing

Psychology and writing, whether we like it or not, are closely woven together for nearly any writer. Whether we're conscious of it or not, we engage in some way with our inner voices whenever we express our ideas.

Practicing mindfulness in the writing process does not mean that you must sit and meditate for extended periods of time. You could try that, of course, if you're interested! But for our purposes, the way to harness mindfulness for writing involves two seemingly simple steps:

- Pay attention to yourself as you write.
- Take responsibility for noticing and ultimately confronting the inner struggles that get in the way of writing in the way you want to write.

These steps can inspire difficult resistances. Fortunately, getting into the habit of noticing and accepting those resistances is part of the process.

You might experiment with strategic mindful pauses during your drafting process. Here are some moments when such pauses might help:

- *If you notice yourself getting restless, bored, or frustrated as you write.* Stop and ask yourself why you feel that way. What's bothering you? What could help you? Is something in the writing itself problematic for you?
- *If you experience a specific issue or tangle in writing an essay.* As you breathe in, imagine fresh energy coming in to help you solve it. As you breathe out, imagine the confusion or stuckness moving out of your body.
- *If you have emotions about what you're writing about.* Acknowledge them. You might release them in a private freewrite, or share them with a friend. Would including those emotions in your essay be useful? If so, you can find a way. If not, how can you best put them aside so you can write the essay?

Sitting quietly with yourself, focusing on being aware and present in the moment helps you develop an inner "parent" of sorts that you can summon to help with your writing.

By "inner parent," I'm not talking about a critic or a judge. I mean the kind of benevolent parent who can help you to assess and deal with whatever's going on. "You are super-angry at that person," that parent might notice, and then ask, "What do you need to make things easier for yourself?" Or they could say, "you have three essays to write in three days. Let's figure out a strategy for doing that." Or "you don't understand this part of the assignment. Whom can you reach out to for help? Or "you haven't been eating or sleeping enough. How about if you take a break before writing more?"

On the way to developing an inner parent like that you will most likely have to confront the other kind of inner voices, the ones that are part of the psychology of many writers—the badgering voices that prevent you from doing your best writing. "You should have started three days ago!" "This writing is terrible!" Instead of helping, such voices increase anxiety and often make you frozen and stuck.

Confronting toxic inner voices can be an important step on the road to developing a helpful inner parent. The more you expose and examine them, the more you can lessen their influence.

Three Kinds of Destructive Inner Voices in the Writing Process

The Relentless Judge: This inner voice scoffs at you as you write, figuratively looking over your shoulder with an expression of contempt. "That doesn't sound very good." "Your argument makes no sense!" "You're too wordy, too choppy, too simplistic." "How did you think this idea was good—it doesn't work!" This voice can become a terrible Radio NST that plagues you, forcing you to do mediocre work because you rush through and stop before you're finished revising, simply because you need to get away from its badgering. Too much of it can prevent you from ever taking yourself seriously as a writer, even if you long to do so, because it won't allow you the inner space to calmly express and rethink your ideas.

The Frantic Anxiety-Producer: This inner voice arises if, say, you haven't done the essay and it's the last minute. It prods you with frantic words designed to increase your anxiousness: "It's getting late!" "You won't be able to finish!" "Why didn't you do this earlier?" That last question might be a useful one to ponder later, but when the paper is due and you are behind, this voice serves only as a torturer. Putting energy into feeling guilty or terrible about yourself drains you unnecessarily.

The Quitter: This inner voice wants to force you out of the present moment of your writing. "All this writing and revising is too hard," it might say. "And it's boring. Just stop and do it later, or tomorrow, or some other time." Have you ever said, "starting tomorrow," or "this weekend," or "this summer," or "next semester," you'll do all your writing perfectly and everything will be great, only to find out that things don't necessarily work out that way once the time comes? That might be because this inner judge is perpetually devoted to taking you away from the process of sitting with your writing *in present time*.

The route to resisting all these inner voices runs through truly accepting your situation without judgment. That means resisting going into the past—what you should have done—or future—what you must do. You can't change the past, and you can't control the future as much as you want to.

Develop your own calm, present-moment inner parent. It will help you proceed more effectively with a writing project, simply by encouraging you to have that powerful experience: being wherever you *actually are*.

STUDENT EXAMPLE
A Student Reflects on Past Doubts about Writing

I felt uncomfortable seeing my own self reflected in my writing. I felt too vulnerable ... I didn't like most of what I wrote ... Teachers all want different things to be focused on in our assigned pieces of writing, and I have been conditioned to only write the way the teacher wants to get a specific grade. My own creativity with writing has sometimes led to my own demise, at least grades wise. When I've been free in my own writing, it's often been too overwhelming ... I do not know if my own issues concerning writing come from a deep-seated insecurity or if I'm actually a bad writer. (ER)

STUDENT EXAMPLE
A Student's Reflection on Accepting Experience As It Is

"We suffer, plain and simple, when we want our experience to be something other than what it is" (Herring 146). This is a simple and profound idea which when grasped could easily alter the trajectory of a life.

When I first read this sentence, it made perfect sense to me and came at a time when I was experiencing what I would describe as suffering. I'd just gotten into an argument with my girlfriend over a disagreement about how we communicated feelings. What should've been a simple back-and-forth had quickly soured and I found myself hurt and upset by the end of it. We suffer, plain and simple, when we want our experience to be something other than what it is. The beauty of this approach to pain and discomfort is that it doesn't wish it away or sweep it under the rug. It doesn't quickly move on to the next topic. I felt upset with the situation and prematurely trying to convince myself otherwise would only exacerbate my suffering. Settling into your experiences, particularly the uncomfortable ones, requires you to wade through ambiguity and pain. It is hardly ever the preferred course of action; however, what lies on the other side is a changed you, one less susceptible to the same ills which caused your initial discomfort. (AN)

Using Mindfulness While Writing

This section proceeds chronologically, addressing how you can use mindfulness in four overall stages of your writing project: before sitting down to write, at the start of writing, in the middle of drafting, and revising. Some of these ideas echo advice I gave you in the rest of this book; I condense it here with a focus on your inner experience.

Before You Begin

In the hours or days before sitting down to write. Let your essay be a seed in your head, and pay attention to the ways it might want to grow. What's the most interesting or exciting thing for you about it? What is it connected to? What, if anything, do you resist in it? Just notice.

If you're reading something you will later write about, be mindful of what's going on in your head as you read. Pay attention, with curiosity, to the thoughts and reactions that occur to you. Write them down.

When it's time to write, arrange your space the way you like it. How can your surroundings help you feel calm and comfortable while writing?

Simply sit for a few moments, noticing your breath, and how your body feels in whatever position it's in.

Survey your inner self. What's going on in you right now? Notice with your non-judgmental witness.

If your head is full of distracting thoughts, set a timer, close your eyes, and count your breath: in one, two, three, four, pause, and then out one, two, three, four. Relax. Notice how the air feels as it moves. Follow it in through your nose, your lungs, and into the bottom of your stomach, feel it stay still for a moment, and then follow its motion as you breathe slowly out. Notice your distracting thoughts without judgment. Imagine them exiting your mind as you breathe out, and breathe in fresh energy for writing.

Open your eyes, and if you feel the need, do a private freewrite. You might be bothered or distracted by something that will get in the way of your focus on the writing project at hand. If so, write to yourself privately about whatever that is. Putting it onto paper or screen can be another mindful way to clear your head.

As You Begin Working on Your Essay

Freewrite on your topic. This can be a good way to begin playing with your essay, and in the process you might give yourself material to go on as you draft it.

Feel free to start your draft in the middle. Many students approach writing an essay by beginning with the introduction and moving systematically from there to the conclusion. Sometimes it works better if you switch it up. Mindfulness can help you reflect on what part of your essay excites you most. Begin there!

Be open to being quirky. The more mindful you are of the particularities of your inner landscapes, the more open you'll be to the kinds of ideas that will lead you to the essays only you can write.

Imagine a child running up to a parent, holding up an oddly shaped rock, and saying, "Look what I found! A star!" Imagine the parent saying, "No, that's not a star, it's a rock! Don't bother me."

Don't unwittingly act as that same kind of unpleasant parent to yourself by crushing your own ideas in the name of "that idea makes no sense." That kind of crushing can happen beyond conscious thought, perhaps when a writer thinks, "I just can't think of anything, I'm stuck," when instead what's subconsciously working overtime is that ideas arise but get struck down immediately by that internal judge who can't be open to the intriguing possibilities of something like an oddly shaped rock.

Freewriting can be a great help in using the "without judgment" element of mindfulness to help you deepen your ideas. If something arises in your regular drafting that seems to "come out of left field," for example, your conscious mind might reject it as inappropriate, silly, unnecessary, or anything else that would spur you to ignore it. However, if you've practiced looking without judgment at your thoughts, you might be surprised by the valuable information that lurks in seemingly throwaway ideas.

While Writing Your Draft

Be mindful of timing when it comes to self-criticism. If you start deleting sentences and changing your mind the minute you start writing you're probably not using your critical muscle in the most useful way. Yes, it is crucial to look at your own writing with a critical eye, even one that's unsparingly so, but *when* you do so is key. Separate the work of your creative and critical muscles.

Timing is everything. In the early stages of your writing your inner parent should help you get your critical muscle out of the way, since it's easiest to gain access to new ideas when you're free not to judge them. Later, your critical muscle will be welcome—as long as its goal is to help your essay get better.

Get into the habit of paying attention to the destructive messages you might give yourself about your writing. These might come out consciously, in the form of your internal voice saying things like, "This is so dumb," or a zillion variations on that theme. But they could also work more subtly, as just a feeling in your body that your conscious mind barely notices.

I tend to feel my self-judgment in my stomach, a sensation of unpleasantness that twists me up inside and makes me stop writing. I often don't think the feeling is related to my writing until I really tune into my internal, mindful listening.

That kind of destructive message might also emerge as an emotion. You might feel inexplicably angry or irritable while writing, and not connect your emotion to your writing unless you take time to ask yourself what's really going on. I've been amazed at times to realize that what's really motivating, say, my annoyance with a friend is the unrelated fact that on some unconscious level I'm feeling bad at the thought that something I'm writing isn't good enough.

If something feels wrong as you're writing, stop and ask yourself why. "What am I feeling about this writing? What am I telling myself about it?" At first, just notice and see what comes up.

You might resist asking such questions about writing, because you just want to get your essay finished. That's understandable, and if not worrying about psychology works for you, go for it.

But the problem is that sometimes you just *can't* finish your essay, even if every part of your conscious mind says, "Just do it, just write!" That's a wonderful idea, but something might stop you cold. Nothing happens. You just stare at your page or screen, or maybe you tell yourself you're just going to check something online for a moment that turns into two hours, and then it's getting late and you've done no writing at all.

Changing any habit is difficult. I might tell myself, "From now on, I'm going to keep this desk perfectly tidy by straightening it up every day," and then do it for a while, but then I get busy and things pile up. I might then think, "That's it! I give up! This desk will never be tidy!" But if I can get myself to look with a mindful, non-judgmental eye I can say, "Ok, so I didn't tidy my desk for two weeks. It's okay. I can't change that, but I can clean it up right now!"

It's the same with writing: non-judgmental attention to what you're actually doing and feeling gives you something to work with. *Right now* you feel that your essay will never work, and maybe you just can't do it right now. But if you accept that and are kind to yourself you might be able to do a little bit tomorrow, or even in ten minutes, and that little bit can inspire you to do more. You might not be able to make it perfect (whatever that means), but no matter what, mindfulness about your feelings will give you more control than a lack of mindfulness.

If you are stuck or suddenly not in the mood to write. Sometimes you don't need to look inward; you can look outward instead. Take a break, go for a walk, write about something else, or do whatever is fun for you. You might feel better when you come back.

When It's Time to Revise

Read your writing aloud. We hear that advice often, but sometimes we reject it—"it takes too much time," we might think, or "it's a waste of energy," or "someone might hear me!" But hearing your words aloud, in your own voice, can be one of the best mindful ways to revise. While listening to yourself, you'll find parts you love and parts that might make you cringe. Can you be honest with yourself about the latter, and revise them so they sound the way you want them to?

Notice how you are critiquing yourself. Whether criticism of your writing comes from yourself or from others, it's only useful when the criticism is productive. Productive criticism means thinking directly about the essay itself: "Does it work to begin that way?" "Is that sentence clear?" "Maybe my thesis needs some rethinking." Unproductive criticism is criticizing yourself as a person: "You're a terrible writer!" "You never organize properly," "You're so stupid for waiting until the last minute," etc. See the difference? Leave unproductive criticism behind.

Be attentive to your instincts. While reading their writing aloud, some students will stop and say, "Oh, that's not right. I have to change it," and then pencil in a note to themselves about how to modify their words. That's a wonderful sign that their instincts are paying good, productive attention.

However, other students might stumble throughout the whole process of reading aloud, repeating the words, "This whole thing is *terrible!*" That's because their instincts about their writing are too entangled with their unproductive inner judge. There's a big difference between a harsh voice that says, "This is terrible," and a thoughtful, critical-muscle voice that says, "This doesn't work, but it could be better if you ..." The latter will make your essay better; the former will get in your way. It can be hard to tell the difference between them, but trusting your deepest instincts will help.

Untangling Inner Critics

I often read my writing aloud while I revise it. As I do so, I sometimes get to parts that make me cringe because something in me says they just sound wrong. That's potentially a beneficial process, but for me it used to be torture.

For a long time, sensing anything "wrong" in my writing had the power to derail my writing completely. A rebellious part of me didn't want to change or revise anything. I was furious at the thought that my writing had flaws and needed work. I couldn't get myself to fix it; instead, I got grumpy, and ended up abandoning my essays way before they were finished.

Mindfulness helped me realize that my frustration was a kind of rebellion against an internal voice in me that criticized everything about my writing. That voice made me feel ashamed of not writing perfectly, and I didn't want to acknowledge that shame, even to myself. So I hid behind feeling super annoyed at whatever person, or voice in me, was telling me to make any changes in what I'd written.

Fortunately, I finally figured out what was going on: I had an inner sense of what really did need to be revised, but instead of being able to listen to it calmly I was getting it tangled up with my harsh, destructive inner critic that insisted that no matter what I did, nothing in my writing would ever be good enough.

I had to disentangle the "good" critic in me, which was made up of my own practical ideas about how my essays could be better, from the destructive one.

Mindfulness helped me to accept the fact that yes, I did need to make changes in what I was writing, and I even knew what those changes were. There was nothing shameful in that—it was simply a part of the process. Realizing that helped me step away from the harsh critic in me as I revised and listen instead to my calmer, more practical instincts that could lead me where I wanted to go.

You too can listen to your instincts about your writing. You have more wisdom in you than you might think.

Judge yourself calmly. No one writes a perfect draft right off the bat— you have to shape and revise your essays before they're finished. Can your benevolent inner parent relax and be productively critical of what you write?

Find your pride. What do you like best in your own essays? What parts are you proud of? Too often, we focus only on the sections of our writing that we think need to be changed. Pay more attention to the parts you like. Admire them. Ask your friends to read them and only tell you what they like about them. Read your work to yourself, and marvel at what a good job you've done.

PART FIVE

Giving and Receiving Feedback in Peer Groups

The Psychology of Feedback

Writing for Readers

Writing can be lonely if you do it only for yourself and your professors.

Students often think the only purpose of sharing writing in school is to have someone help you "fix" it. But one of the best ways to inspire yourself as a writer is to share your writing with other people simply for the pleasure and satisfaction of having them hear and respond to whatever you have to say.

This part is about peer feedback designed to help you improve your writing, but I encourage you to enjoy your peers' writing along with critiquing it. And when others respond to your writing, be open to the ways in which they are responding to your interesting ideas.

What Is Peer Feedback, and Why Does It Make Some People Nervous?

Peer feedback is commentary on a peer's paper. It differs from commentary by the professor, or even by, say, a student working in your institution's

writing center. The latter might be your age, and thus a "peer" in other contexts, but in their capacity as a tutor they are higher in the hierarchy than you are; when it comes to your tutoring session with them, the two of you do not have an equal relationship.

In what I'm calling peer feedback, the relationships are equal. Peers are usually in the same class. They work in groups of two, three, or four, and no one in the group has more authority than anyone else. Outside of a class, they could be any group of friends or colleagues who share their work as equals, with everyone sharing and no one in the "teacher" role.

Participating in peer groups has many benefits beyond helping you with your writing. Job recruiters often say "the ability to work well in groups" is one of the top qualities they look for in candidates. And learning to give effective feedback helps you cultivate your ability to read with a thoughtful, critical eye, noticing nuances you might previously have ignored.

Yes, peer feedback groups on writing help you develop useful life skills. But this part is primarily about how very valuable they can be for your writing itself, both when you respond and when others respond to you.

Peer feedback sessions should be comfortable, useful, and fun. Why, then, do they so often make people nervous? Probably because even when you are among friendly peers, comparisons and judgments can get in the way.

EXERCISE 1
What Is Your Experience with Peer Responding?

Write about the following questions, and then share them with a peer or the class:

- Have you shared your writing in peer groups in previous classes?
- How do you feel about peer response groups?
- What are you like as a responder and/or what would you like to be like?
- Can you think of specific feedback someone has given you on your writing? What kinds of feedback do you like best? Find most useful?

Inadequate vs. Superior

Feeling inadequate. "Her writing is *so good*," a student will sometimes tell me about a peer, "I can't think of anything to tell her that could possibly help her writing." Students with that attitude usually tend to be quiet in a peer group. If they must speak, they say things like, "Don't change a thing, it really works!" or look for very minor points, like "maybe change that comma to a period." While their own essay is being discussed they might sit there, blank faced, writing things down, and later incorporate every comment, no matter what, into their revision. They might even "inexplicably" miss class the next time feedback groups are scheduled.

Feeling superior. "I only want to talk about my essay with *you*," another kind of student will say to me. "Since you're the professor giving me the grade, your feedback is better than theirs." When they must participate in a feedback group, such students tend to assume that their thoughts are always correct: "that part doesn't work," "add this here," "change that; it doesn't work at *all*," which often, understandably, may alienate any fellow students they haven't been able to convince of their own superiority.

Dismissing a Common Misconception

Before going further, let's get rid of the misconception people sometimes have about giving peer feedback on essays: that it is simply charity work, aimed at helping writers who aren't as good as we are. No, the main purpose of peer feedback groups is to help *all* writers in two important ways:

⊙ *They help you begin to see your own drafts as others see them.* Our emotions often get in our way when we read our own writing—at times we love it and don't want to change a thing; at other times we hate it and think everything about it is awful. Seeing our essay through others' eyes inevitably gives us some kind of a different take.

- They allow you to *exercise your critical muscle* in a more neutral setting than you have when working on your own writing. Looking at someone else's essay is like going to a gym for strengthening our own critical muscle. Unruffled by personal connections to the material, that muscle gets a chance to strengthen its backbends and muscle tone in peace. After stretching your muscle by looking critically at someone else's writing you inevitably go back to your own with fresher eyes. You stand back from your work a little more easily and thus revise more productively; hopefully you've also made a friend or two.

These benefits are why many writers get together often to share writing—when done effectively, it's a win-win situation for all concerned.

EXERCISE 2
Respond to a Fragment of Writing

Here is a section of a freewrite written by a student:

> Unfortunately, I feel that I am always thinking. This is immensely helpful in school, as I almost never have a shortage of ideas, but in my personal life it can be challenging. Overthinking can lead to anguish if it is not managed properly. This is something I've made immense progress with, although it is a journey I am still undergoing. (GK)

Imagine that the student wants to develop this little piece into a longer, reflective essay. What might you say? Do a freewrite about your thoughts, perhaps incorporating answers to some of the questions below:

- What do you like about this?
- What do you want to hear more about?
- What else would you say to the student to help with the process of developing their thoughts?

After you have written on your own for five minutes, share your writing with a classmate and discuss. Did you each respond in the same way, or did you go in different directions? What conclusions and questions arose about how to respond to writing?

Fear Can Get in the Way

I have noticed two kinds of fears arising in peer feedback groups, and both have to do with being judged.

Fear of being judged as a not-so-good writer. Sharing writing is a double-edged sword. The intimacy of communicating with readers is beautiful, but being seen means you're out there to be judged, which means you could be misunderstood, or dismissed. Being judged in any context can be difficult, but writing is especially close to our hearts, and it's important for peer feedback groups to acknowledge vulnerabilities, and be sensitive about how their comments are received.

However, being careful about commenting, and striving to nurture and respect the writer, certainly does not mean that you should only say "good things" in a peer group. Not at all! As I'll explain, there are ways to exercise your critical muscle as a responder that both respect other writers and dig in to help them revise extensively.

Fear of not giving good feedback on your classmates' work. This fear involves another kind of self-exposure that can lead you to feel judged by others—the exposure of how good a responder you are or aren't.

In peer groups with other professional writers, I've sometimes had the sense that everyone is vying to be the person who offers the best, most insightful comment. That competition is unspoken—most people would never admit to competing for such a thing—but it can be oppressive, both for responders and for the writer being responded to.

Just as peer groups don't work well if they become competitions for who is the best writer, they also don't work well as contests to see who the best responder is. It can be embarrassing not to know what to say about someone's writing. But no matter what kind of a writer you are, you can learn to be a good responder if you put aside your competitive urges and focus instead on the essay draft at hand.

"Tear It Apart!"

Despite any inner hesitation, many writers want responders to "dig in" to their writing. "Tear it apart!" they say. "I don't mind, I can take it—I just want to make my essay better!"

It's rarely that easy.

What does the request to tear it apart really mean? The most obvious sentiment behind it is that you are willing to work hard on your writing, and you don't want responders to let concern for your feelings get in the way of telling you about its flaws. You can take it! Maybe your writing has been met before with comments like "it's good," which you detest. "That kind of 'nice' comment doesn't help me with anything!" you might scoff.

I get that. I too want my writing to be good, and in theory, I'd like readers to just tell me what's wrong with it so I can fix it. However, I've learned that there are two significant kinds of problems with that goal. One is practical and one is personal.

Practical Problems with "Tear It Apart"

The assumption behind tear it apart is that composing an essay is like building a building. If it isn't "working," it's because maybe the foundation beam isn't strong enough, or the windows haven't been installed properly. Any expert in building will notice such mistakes by surveying the building and can help the builder adjust so the building will "work," meaning it will stand up on its own and function properly.

To an extent, that metaphor works with writing. An essay could certainly "not work," and could even "fall apart" if it's not properly constructed. Handing in a freewrite and calling it an essay is an example of that: it's not working as an essay yet, it's not standing—it's more like a pile of wood and cement without any structure to hold it up.

However, there's also a big problem with thinking of an essay as a metaphorical building that can be fixed. When it comes to a building, there is a clear scientific answer about whether, and how, it can stand up. All the experts who look at the beams will basically do the same assessment, because their opinion is based on the laws of physics.

With an essay, though, experts can, and will, disagree. The world of literary and arts criticism is a testament to that—learned critics often have deeply different views about the value of one essay (or movie or song or poem or performance or sculpture, etc.) in relation to the next. So when a responder to an essay says with certainty, and many do, "This works," and, "That does not work," they can't possibly speak with the same authority that the construction engineer does when looking at the beams of a house. They are speaking of *opinion*, more akin to someone liking, or disliking, the shape or color of the house, not its structure.

Your demand that I tear your essay apart is often the demand that I tell you what's wrong with it as though I have the definitive answer. I don't! No one does. Professors act as experts, it's our job, and yes, we do have a lot of expertise. But the assessments we make about essays depend on many factors, some of which we ourselves might not even be completely aware of. When we grade essays, we do our best to articulate what our standards are—to some, having a clear thesis is paramount; to others, a clear voice is the greatest value; others see close reading of texts as crucial; still others look primarily at how the writer makes use of evidence to develop an argument; and that's only the beginning of a long list of qualities that go into judgments of writing. It's unlikely that you would find any set of readers, even professors in the same field, who would all agree on the specific balance among such qualities when it comes to what is and isn't "wrong" with your essay.

So it's not very effective simply to ask someone to tear it apart, because there are many ways to do so, and not all will work for you. Does tear it apart mean "tell me how you would write this if you were me?" Often responders are happy to provide that information—they may even do so without thinking because they think the way they would write it is the only way to write the essay. But they're wrong about that. It's your essay, not theirs.

Asking readers to tear your essay apart does mean that you don't want them to be superficial and say only good things. But what in particular is it that you really want? Let's look deeper.

Personal Problems with "Tear It Apart"

Students who demand that responders tear their writing apart are often surprisingly unhappy when the feedback includes ideas like, "this part doesn't work, get rid of it," or "... that part is good," or "move the other part to page two and change the introduction," or "you have some awkward sentences," or "add more examples."

Ouch! Was that what you wanted when you asked me to tear it apart? Perhaps not.

When people who say "tear it apart," *do* in fact mean they want you to "fix" their draft by inserting your own solutions for whatever is "wrong," they most likely don't have much of a sense of ownership over their own writing. They want you to fix it so they don't have to worry about it anymore. If you want to tear down whatever part of their house they've built and rebuild it with your own, better materials, no problem!

However, rebuilding a peer's essay is not the job of a peer responder.

In school, or with anyone who takes their own writing seriously, the point of feedback is to help the writer write a better version of the essay only they can write. As a responder, and also as a professor, I want to help you build the house *you* want, not to seize control of your house and build it myself in my own way. Even if I'm a wonderful builder, you won't feel good telling people you built the house if I've taken it over. You'll feel much better if you've built it your way, and my job is to help you do *that*.

What "Tear It Apart" Really Means

When serious writers say, "tear it apart," they don't usually mean they want you to build their house, or their essay. What they want you to do is to *think with them in depth about their writing*, to get into their head with them and poke around, to leave your own tastes aside so you can *be with them* in the nitty gritty of the kinds of things writers always have to do: fiddle over details, reconsider the structure, come up with wild suggestions and possibilities, and otherwise find ways to develop and revise.

There's nothing like getting feedback that works, which happens when your responder *gets* you, and finds good ways to nudge you toward more clarity about what you're trying to say.

How does a student peer responder do that, exactly? Won't it take way too much time? And how hard is it? It takes time, yes, and involves work, but I'm here to tell you that it's not too hard, and it doesn't take too much time. In fact, it can be a lot of fun!

Being a Peer Responder

It's not as hard as you might think to be an effective peer responder, though it might be hard in ways that are different from what you thought. It's not your job to be the teacher/judge who knows "the answer" about the essay under consideration. You don't have to be "as good" a writer, whatever that means, as the person you're responding to, and you can get excellent feedback yourself from someone you might not consider to be "as good" a writer as you are.

What does "good" mean when it comes to writing anyway? You might become preoccupied with it in a peer-feedback setting—"Who is good?" "Who is less good?" "Who is bad?" "How do I stack up?" Many of us ask some version of those questions, at least in our own minds, when we're in a peer feedback group. But I advise you to notice and then let such questions slide off you. They get in the way of making your feedback work as well as it could.

It's understandable if your first reaction to a peer's draft is, "it's fine as is" or "it has problems, but I have no idea what to do about them, or even exactly what they are." But your job as a peer responder is to go past such reactions.

The key is to look more closely at the essay to discover what gave you whatever initial reaction you had. You can start with, "What in *particular*

did the writer do that you think is good?" or "What part doesn't seem quite right, and why?" Give the writer the one thing they could never give themselves—the knowledge of how someone who isn't them reads their work.

Comments that seem unusual to the responder can be surprisingly effective in helping us revise our work. In his book *Writing with Power*, Peter Elbow gives useful and sometimes eccentric suggestions of ways to respond to writing. For example, "if this essay were a piece of clothing, what would it be?" Students often laugh at such a question, but think about it: Would an essay that's a tuxedo be different from one that's a ratty blue sweater? Does contemplating that metaphor tell you something about the two essays?

You don't have to look at essays in terms of clothing, though it could be interesting to try. You might also investigate Elbow's other prompts—what weather is the essay like? What kind of person?—if you want to stretch yourself beyond "this works" and "that doesn't work" types of feedback.

Trying to articulate any impressions that come into your head when you read someone's writing can touch off thinking that the writer might find useful, as long as your focus remains on the writing itself. Does my essay need to be more of a tuxedo than an old sweater? Is it too much like a tuxedo? Your comments on that could potentially help me revise.

An Aside: "Everyone Switched Emotions"

One of my sisters used to be part of a downtown modern dance scene in New York City. She choreographed performances in which dancers would do unpredictable things—shriek, wear bizarre costumes, chase each other around the stage, etc. One day my mother came into the city from the suburbs to see one of my sister's dances. I sat with her, wondering how she'd react since she'd never seen a quirky "downtown" performance before.

My mother paid close attention, laughing along with the audience when my sister shouted out random words as she danced, such as, "imagine. Imagine? Imagine!" My mother was riveted.

"What did you think, Mom?" I asked when it was over.

"It was ... different," she said and wouldn't add more.

Later, my sister asked her what she'd thought. "I can't possibly say," my mother said, "I don't know anything about this kind of dance."

That annoyed my sister. "But what was it like for you? What did you see?"

My mother thought about it. "I really liked the way everyone switched emotions," she said. "It gave me a feeling of happiness, but then the guy in red was so menacing!"

My sister laughed. "I love that you saw him that way," she said. "I wasn't really thinking of him as menacing, but now you're making me think he should emphasize that part more. And the idea of crazy, quick-switching emotions—that's what I was hoping the audience would see, thank you!"

"*Really?*" My mother asked, quite pleased and surprised that her comment had made more sense than she would have thought.

Similar things happen with writing responses—when you take the risk of articulating your actual reactions, you'll be surprised at how helpful they can become.

Framing Is Important

Peer responders should keep in mind that it's not just what you say in your feedback, it's how you say it. The following four sections discuss some rules you might follow when you want your feedback to *dig in* but *not take over*.

Go from "Macro" to "Micro"

Before getting into details, start your feedback session by giving the writer your sense of the essay as a whole—as in, "Okay, this is an argumentative essay about why religious issues dominated higher education in New England in the nineteenth century. You respond to X's theory of Y, by arguing that Z." For this part, you should be as objective as possible as a responder, describing what you see.

After a general statement like that, begin to examine the pieces of the essay considering what you see as its overall plan. "On page two I kind of lost you for a moment, but then you seem to have gotten back on track at the top of page three ..." still moving from larger issues—maybe the order of ideas or paragraphs, or the writer's choice and use of evidence, or their overall voice—to smaller ones, like the coherence of individual paragraphs—and lastly to specific sentences.

If you focus in on something relatively minor too soon, you could get bogged down in something the writer might eventually change or delete. It can be more challenging to take responsibility first for describing the essay as a whole, but it will be far more useful to the writer if you start there.

Present Your Criticisms in a Way That Allows the Writer to Do Something about Them

Imagine these two comments on your draft:

- "This draft is a mess—very disorganized."
- "When I read your first paragraph, I thought you were going to go in X direction. But when I got to your second paragraph, you brought in Y, which made me think this was an entirely different paper—I couldn't find X anywhere. X came up again in the third paragraph, but your discussion of Y had disappeared."

Both reactions point to the same problem, but which would you rather have as a response from a peer? A student might interpret the first one as "tearing the essay apart," but they still wouldn't know what to do about it. They probably already knew the essay was disorganized.

The second comment, what Elbow calls, "telling the story of your thinking," could be much more useful in helping you figure out how to restructure. It would lead to useful questions the writer might productively ask themself:

- *Did I have a reason for switching to the topic of Y in my second paragraph?* If not, maybe that paragraph doesn't belong there. But what should I do with the topic of Y? I don't want to get rid of it, or do I?

- *Maybe Y needs to be more of a part of my thesis?* Let's say X is "whales are in danger." And Y is "people have been shooting wolves." *If the writer had gotten the first comment above*, "this is disorganized," they might decide they have to get rid of either whales or wolves. *However, the second comment above could* cause them to realize that if they want to include Y, they have to do so more effectively. For example, they might decide to revamp the thesis to something like, "many animals that were once threatening to humans are now in danger themselves from humans." That does potentially include X and Y.

- *Okay, but is there some other way of incorporating both X and Y?* "I don't want to slide into a boring structure that simply says, 'here are a few examples of the same thing,'" the writer might say. "I want my essay to be more alive. So maybe my revamped thesis could be something like, 'whales are in danger; our unengaged attitude toward them and other animals needs to shift.' Hmm, I like that. Maybe my essay should be all about whales, and wolves don't belong? But wait, I can bring in wolves as part of the conclusion, to show an alternative example."

Thus a writer could take those relatively simple, critical observations from the second comment above and use them as the basis for productive thinking about the essay. Once they understand why a reader is confused, it's their job to figure out what needs to change in the essay to make their point as clear as possible.

Opine, Don't Evaluate

As a peer-responder, keep the fact foremost in your mind that it's not your job to be the judge or to tell the writer what to do. Of course, you'll make private judgments in your own mind as you read your peers' writing, but take the time to frame your descriptions of those judgments as opinion, rather than fact. It might seem like an unnecessary distinction, but it isn't: how you phrase your feedback makes a huge difference in how people receive what you say.

A Word about Grammar and Syntax

As you know, it's essential that finished essays are grammatically correct. Little will alienate readers more than an essay containing grammatical mistakes and sentences that don't make proper sense.

Knowing that, responders sometimes go straight to grammar, the most "micro" of issues, as the first thing to comment on when they read an essay. That's understandable—pointing to grammatical errors is the closest we can get to applying an objective standard to someone's writing. There are fixed rules about how to use a semicolon or construct a sentence, and for the most part experts would agree about what is grammatically right or wrong.

When it comes to feedback on writing, though, it's important to be strategic if you want to help someone with their grammar.

Here are four rules about responding to a writer's grammar or syntax:

- *Ignore it if the draft is at an early stage.* When writers aren't sure what they are saying in their essay overall, looking at grammar mistakes can derail them. Some peer responders have an almost unbearable impulse to take a pen and revise all of another student's grammar. Here are some problems with that strategy:
  - » The writer might not know exactly what they want to say. Stopping to worry about grammar errors can prevent them from moving forward.
  - » You might not know the correct grammar rules yourself—leave that to the professor. I've seen many errors in "corrections" by students on peers' essays. But even if you are a grammar expert, it won't help a writer for you to point out errors too soon.

> » The writer might end up getting rid of the section that includes the changes you make.

- *Even with an essay that is more developed, leave grammar errors for last.* They represent the "icing on the cake." The writer must get the cake of the essay baked before worrying about the details of the icing.

- *If you are responding to a writer who is not a native English speaker,* holding back can be especially difficult, especially if your peer asks you to "fix" their grammar. But the above rules still apply—the larger picture of the essay is the first step. If you see a repeated error, you might help them with it, but as a peer responder your job is not to be a copyeditor who corrects all the grammar.

- *If the writer has finished the essay and wants you to read for grammar mistakes, that's fine. But you might do so by,* say, putting a symbol in the margin when you see an error as opposed to making the changes yourself. You may or not be correct about how the sentence could be improved.

General Process for In-Class Group Work with Drafts

The Structure of a Typical Exercise

- Meet in small groups (two to four).

- Begin by giving each student a chance to introduce their draft:
  - » Where they are in the process.
  - » What they are working on/struggling with/unsure about.
  - » Any questions for the group.

- *Exchange papers,* whether paper copies or online.

- *Everyone reads the other essays* with the writer's questions in mind, and *writes answers to a selection of the prompts below.* This writing-comments part is crucial, because it gets each responder's raw reactions down on paper, before they shift and change through discussion. Rethinking those reactions is an inevitable and useful part of the discussion, but it's very useful for the writer to know what readers thought privately on first reading too.

- After everyone has read, *have a conversation as a group*, talking about one essay at a time. The groups should encourage each writer to respond to the feedback, and to talk through their ideas and plans for revising.

Further Advice for Groups

- *Students might read each other's papers the night before*, write notes, and then come to class ready to discuss them.

- *Alternatively, students could read their papers aloud to the group*, followed by discussion of each student's paper before moving to the next. Responders should write privately at least for a few minutes before the group begins talking, to collect their own raw reactions before discussion.

- *If students are reading each other's work on the spot, it's important for everyone to finish reading and writing about the draft before the discussion begins.* If you have finished reading the other essays and someone else in your group isn't finished yet, you might have the impulse to start discussing a paper privately before the other group member is ready. Resist that—*the purpose of discussing essays as a group is for the group as a whole to talk together.* It makes a difference when two people discuss your essay as opposed to one, because readers can have different views, and disagreements can be useful for the writer to hear.

- *Don't be afraid of disagreement among responders.* In fact, welcome it! Sometimes students feel they are "wrong" if they have a comment that disagrees with another responder's. No! Just put it out there for the writer, and help them figure out how they might make use of the disagreement.

- *Don't think your comment is "wrong" if the writer rejects it.* I've found that some of the most useful comments on my writing are those I disagree with. They help me figure out what I do *not* want to do, which leads me to a better understanding of what I do want.

- *The discussion is usually the most important part.* Writers sometimes unthinkingly blurt things out in discussion that might end up working well in their essay. For example, in discussing a personal essay about living in California, a writer might say something like, "That was even before my dad was a surfer." The group could say, "Your dad was a surfer? That belongs in your essay!" Group conversations can foster those kinds of revelations—be open to them!

Advice for Responding to Peer-Feedback on *Your* Writing

The first thing to remember when receiving feedback from peers is that on some level all we really want when someone reads our writing is for them to say, "Wow! Don't change a thing! This is *absolutely perfect* the way it is!" Of course, we will virtually never get that response from a good feedback group. Unfortunately, our drafts can always be improved.

So steel yourself—your peers are going to say things that require you to do some revision. Once you get past your flickers of disappointment about that, be as open as you can to whatever they are saying. Keep in mind that they are giving you *feedback* and not *directions*—you don't have to revise your essay to conform to their wishes, but hearing what they say, even if you don't like it, will inevitably push you to think differently about what you wrote.

It's understandable that sometimes writers get defensive when they hear feedback. "No, you don't understand, you just didn't get what I was *doing*!" you might want to wail when listening to someone's take on your essay. Note reactions like that in yourself and try to keep them to yourself. Remember, your peers are trying to help. If you don't find their feedback useful or insightful, it's your right to nod, smile, and ignore it. On the other hand, there might be some truth in feedback you resist—at least consider that.

If responders disagree with each other about something in your writing, you don't have to resolve their conflict. Note it, and either discuss it on the spot or tell them you'll think about it later. You might be surprised to find that the conflict itself might spur your thinking about your essay in a useful way.

Feel free to ask your peers more questions once they get going on their responses. Even questions of the "do you think I should ..." variety can work if you take the answers as information, and don't just blindly follow them.

Keep your pen in hand or your computer open during your feedback session and write down anything that seems remotely interesting or worthwhile for you. Writers often forget some of the most productive things people say to them in feedback groups.

Prompts for Peer Responders

The goal of these prompts, which are variations on some of Elbow and Belanoff's advice for responding, is to help you think with the writer about their draft, to encourage them to explore other angles on it, and to nudge them toward other possibilities for developing their essay. In other words, they offer some ways to "tear it apart" productively. Each blank space invites you to write not just a few words, but as many sentences as you like.

- *I like the way you* _____. It's useful to begin your response to any paper with this statement. Writers feel good when they hear what you like, and you can find something you like in any piece of writing.

Prompts for Responding to Freewrites or Drafts at the Early Stages in the Process

- *In one sentence, I hear you saying that* _____. It might sound obvious to you to tell the writer what you hear them saying. But writers are often surprised by what different responders hear. They will learn a lot from the nuances among what different peer-responders say.

- *I notice* _____. This prompt invites you to respond to any individual part of the draft. It can be a good place to start if your first reaction to the draft is simply that you think it is "good" and you aren't sure what to say about it. If you begin with what in particular you think is good, you'll be on your way to saying more.

- *I want to hear more about* _____. One caveat: you might want to hear more about something for your own reasons, as in, "oh, you're from those mountains? Do you know any cool hikes to go on?" If the question is for you and not for the paper, save it to ask after the peer-responding work is done. For now, the question is what you want to know more about *for the sake of the essay.*

- *To me, this seems to want to be about* _____. This might seem like an odd thing to observe at first. How could an essay *want* something? But you might have an answer to this question, for example, when the writer mentions something in passing that hints at interesting ideas that might in fact "want" to be more of the overall focus.

- *To me, what seems to be lurking here is* _____. This is related to the previous prompt: What is not quite said but somehow present? For example, in a personal essay about how wonderful someone is, you might sense that some annoyance is "lurking." Point that out, but also let it go if the writer rejects that direction.

- *I feel the most energy when you* _____ *because* _____. This invites you as a responder to point to a section of the text that seems to you to be really "clicking."

- *I lose sight of where you're going when* _____. Don't be afraid to point out places where the writer seems less engaged. Then listen for what they might tell you about their own thoughts about those places and help them figure a way out.

- *This makes me think or wonder about* _____. This question invites you to connect the essay to another question or idea outside of it. It can be useful for the writer to hear your various associations.

- *I have a question about* _____. Feel free to ask, especially if your goal is to understand something in the essay.

Prompts for a Draft that Is Already Taking Shape As an Essay and Seems to Be on Its Way Toward Completion

I say "seems" here, because when a writer thinks the essay is almost complete, the feedback they get can make them realize that they want to do more with it, perhaps including making dramatic shifts in the overall form or takeaway idea. Your goal with this set of prompts is to respond in a way that either confirms the near-completion of an essay, perhaps offering suggestions for final tweaks, or encourages the writer to consider potential weaknesses, or areas that could be dramatically improved.

All of the above prompts could potentially be useful at this later stage. But I also add the following:

- *I like* _____ *about the way you have written this.* Note a specific strategy the writer used.

- *Here's what I notice about your overall structure*: _____. Take a bird's eye view of the essay, and in one sentence, describe what you see. This could be along the lines of, "Your thesis is that X, and you develop it by explaining Y, which leads you to Z, and then by the end you're making the point that B." Or, "Your personal essay uses the concept of X to explore your feelings about Y," etc.

- *For me, this structure might work better if you* _____. This prompt asks for a suggestion. Beginning with "for me" moves it away from the idea that the writer must make the change you suggest. But if you can explain exactly why you think, say, "For me, your essay might work better if you take that second paragraph on page two and make it the introduction," you might help the writer make a useful shift.

- *The genre of this essay seems to me to be X but you seem to shift into a different genre on page* _____. Most likely, this comment points at an inconsistency that the writer should remedy by making sure the genre of the essay is consistent. On the other hand, their shift might be deliberate, and hearing of your confusion might help the writer clarify or otherwise make the shift more understandable.

- *I notice* _____ *about the way you incorporate evidence from texts or elsewhere.* This is an important observation about an essay moving to completion. How does the writer introduce the evidence and discuss it afterward? Does the length of a quote seem right? Do they take the quote out of context? Do they need to say more about their reading of the quote or reference?

- *I lose sight of what you're saying (or even, I feel bored) when* _____. It's hard to tell someone you find them boring! But it's not the writer who is boring, it's just that part of their essay. The writer might be bored by that part as well, and now you can talk about how to make it less boring—maybe by leaving it out altogether, or by livening it up.

> ### An Aside: Paragraph Unity
>
> High school students are sometimes taught to use a separate paragraph for each example in their essays. In college and university classes, you usually have more freedom to experiment with your paragraphs.
>
> There is no fixed rule for what has to go into a paragraph, aside from the fact that each paragraph should work as a whole. You could write a paragraph that is only one sentence long, if it's a sentence you want to emphasize, or you can break up a longer paragraph into separate parts.

Here's what I notice about paragraph unity: _____. This kind of comment is not useful if the draft is at an early stage, but it can be crucial in a later draft. Look at an essay's paragraphs individually in addition to reading them as part of the essay. Does the first sentence of the paragraph lead you to its main subject? Does it build on whatever has come before it? Is the point of each paragraph clear throughout? Does it develop an idea? Is it overly long, and would you suggest breaking it up?

Final Thoughts about Feedback

Peer groups are social and work best when writers feel open and relaxed with each other. Make sure you know everyone's name in your group, and feel free to engage in a few minutes of chatting at the start of your session. That's not a waste of time—it makes a difference in responding when you develop at least some degree of camaraderie in the group before you get to work.

Pay attention to group dynamics:

- Does one person do all the talking?
- Does someone seem overly shy or intimidated by other group members?
- Does one person's essay get all the attention and another's barely any at all?
- Does the group allow time for the writer to respond to feedback, followed by some back-and-forth with everyone?
- What can you do as a group member to make the group work better?
- Is the group enjoying each other?

Becoming aware of such dynamics is a good way to work toward more effective, and fun, group experiences. The first step is simply for you as a group member to pay attention to your own role in the group. Then pay attention to your thoughts about the group's interactions. The next step, only when you feel comfortable, is for the whole group to discuss how you work together. Feel free also to share ideas privately with your instructor, who might be able to help you solve problems that arise with your interpersonal work. Enjoy the process!

Works Cited

Butler, Judith. *Gender Trouble: Feminism and the Subversion of Identity*. Routledge, 2006.

Caulfield, Michael. *Web Literacy for Student Fact-Checkers*. Pressbooks.pub. Accessed 20 April 2023.

Chemaly, Soraya. *Rage Becomes Her: The Power of Women's Anger*. Simon & Schuster, 2019.

Daum, Meghan. "Music Is My Bag." *My Misspent Youth*, Open City Books, 2001, pp. 137–54.

Elbow, Peter. *Writing with Power: Techniques for Mastering the Writing Process*. Oxford UP, 1998.

Elbow, Peter, and Pat Belanoff. *Sharing and Responding*. Random House, 1989.

Ferrante, Elena. *In the Margins: On the Pleasures of Reading and Writing*. Europa Editions, 2022.

Gardner, Howard. *Frames of Mind: The Theory of Multiple Intelligences*. Basic Books, 2011.

Herring, Laraine. *Writing Begins with the Breath: Embodying Your Authentic Voice*. Shambhala Press, 2007.

Johnson, Charles. *Turning the Wheel: Essays on Buddhism and Writing*. Scribner, 2007.

Lamott, Anne. "Shitty First Drafts." *Bird by Bird: Some Instructions on Writing and Life*, Pantheon, 1994, pp. 21–27.

Lopate, Phillip. "Against Joie de Vivre." *The Art*, pp. 716–31.

—, ed. *The Art of the Personal Essay: An Anthology from the Classical Era to the Present*. Anchor, 1997.

—. "My Drawer." *Getting Personal*, Basic Books, 2003, pp. 91–94.

—. "On the Necessity of Turning Oneself into a Character." *To Show and to Tell: The Craft of Literary Nonfiction*, Free Press, 2013, pp. 17–25.

Morano, Michele. "In the Subjunctive Mood." *Grammar Lessons: Translating a Life in Spain*, U of Iowa P, 2014, pp. 25–38.

Nhat Hanh, Thich. *Silence: The Power of Quiet in a World Full of Noise.* HarperOne, 2015.

Orwell, George. "Such, Such Were the Joys." Lopate, *The Art*, pp. 269–302.

Sanders, Scott Russell. "Under the Influence." Lopate, *The Art*, pp. 733–44.

Self, Will. *Psychogeography*. Bloomsbury, 2007.

Shōnagon, Sei. "Hateful Things." Lopate, *The Art*, pp. 24–28.

Smith, Zadie. "Joy." *Best American Essays 2014*, ed. John Jeremiah Sullivan, Houghton Mifflin Harcourt, 2014, pp. 145–51.

Woolf, Virginia. *Mrs. Dalloway*. Mariner Books Classics, 1990.

—. "Street Haunting." Lopate, *The Art*, pp. 256–65.

—. *A Writer's Diary*. Signet, 1968.

Image Credits

Page 10:   Aaron Burden, unsplash.com/photos/yo2jEX_BoOo

Page 14:   Edgar Chaparro, unsplash.com/photos/sHfo3WOgGTU

Page 16:   Brad Neathery, unsplash.com/photos/XrSzacdYbtQ

Page 25:   Andrea Piacquadio, pexels.com/photo/
            woman-in-red-t-shirt-looking-at-her-laptop-3755761

Page 31:   Stephanie LeBlanc, unsplash.com/photos/SVwOposMxHY

Page 35:   Andrea Piacquadio, pexels.com/photo/
            thoughtful-woman-writing-in-notebook-at-home-3769013

Page 41:   A Perry, unsplash.com/photos/OjhSUsHUIYM

Page 49:   Dari lli, unsplash.com/photos/zf8yjaSHMis

Page 52:   Badal Gyawali, unsplash.com/photos/vibpIZgKPSQ

Page 65:   Zen Chung, pexels.com/photo/smiling-multiracial-
            students-working-on-project-together-5538593

Page 66:   Nikola Jovanovic, unsplash.com/photos/OBok3F8buKY

Page 73:   Pedro Carballo, unsplash.com/photos/oFnzIf47j8I

Page 83:   Tima Miroshnichenko, pexels.com/photo/a-college-student-
            reading-a-book-while-sitting-on-the-stairs-9572703

Page 87:   cottonbro studio, pexels.com/photo/
            woman-holding-a-magnifying-glass-6491797

Page 93:   Greta Hoffman, pexels.com/photo/concentrated-black-drag-
            queen-applying-mascara-on-eyelashes-7676001

Page 97:   Andrea Piacquadio, pexels.com/photo/
            clever-female-student-reading-book-in-library-3808060

Page 98:   Craig Adderley, pexels.com/photo/
            man-sitting-on-sofa-reading-book-1467564

Page 99:   Theo, pexels.com/photo/laptop-on-table-beside-mug-3414792

Page 101:   Anete Lusina, pexels.com/photo/
            pensive-ethnic-woman-reading-book-on-street-5239599

Page 104:   Mikhail Nilov, pexels.com/photo/
            male-students-reading-book-in-the-library-9158712
Page 106:   Klaudia Lorenc, pexels.com/photo/
            close-up-of-a-bay-horse-16884193
Page 117:   Ivan Samkov, pexels.com/photo/
            two-men-studying-together-5676678
Page 119:   Tima Miroshnichenko, pexels.com/photo/
            person-holding-pen-writing-on-white-paper-8764625
Page 121:   Keira Burton, pexels.com/photo/multiracial-students-studying-
            on-netbook-with-notebook-on-steps-6147398
Page 125:   RF._.studio, pexels.com/photo/
            photo-of-woman-reading-books-3059654
Page 128:   Mizuno K, pexels.com/photo/
            bored-woman-at-an-office-desk-12911180
Page 130:   Ivan Samkov, pexels.com/photo/
            close-up-of-woman-taking-notes-4240575
Page 135:   Clay Banks, unsplash.com/photos/GX8KBbVmC6c
Page 137:   Pixabay, pexels.com/photo/
            people-sitting-inside-well-lit-room-159740
Page 139:   cottonbro studio, pexels.com/photo/
            woman-in-gray-crew-neck-t-shirt-reading-magazine-4778411
Page 143:   Mikhail Nilov, pexels.com/photo/
            man-in-black-suit-jacket-using-silver-laptop-9159002
Page 146:   Marcio Skull, pexels.com/photo/
            statue-of-a-man-with-chain-13569998
Page 149:   cottonbro studio, pexels.com/photo/woman-in-white-long-
            sleeve-shirt-sitting-beside-woman-in-red-shirt-4778621
Page 155:   Keira Burton, pexels.com/photo/
            multiethnic-students-studying-together-in-fall-park-6146971
Page 159:   RF._.studio, pexels.com/photo/woman-in-black-tank-top-and-
            black-pants-sitting-on-concrete-floor-3820312
Page 166:   Tatiana Syrikova, pexels.com/photo/curious-little-girl-in-warm-
            clothing-walking-on-winter-beach-3932879
Page 167:   Thea, unsplash.com/photos/w8kevFdCcTs
Page 171:   Mental Health America (MHA), pexels.com/photo/
            man-holding-his-head-sitting-outside-5543181
Page 183:   Monstera, pexels.com/photo/
            diverse-classmates-talking-to-each-other-after-studies-6238082

Index

academic essays, 12–13
analysis, 12, 102, 126–27
argument, 12, 100, 126–27, 144–45

"before and after" essay structure,
    57–58, 62–63
boredom, 128–29
Butler, Judith, 92–94

Chemaly, Soraya, 74
chronological essay structure, 57
citation, 109, 114–15, 154
clichés, 38–40
close readings, 102
conclusions, 76–78, 115, 149–51
creative nonfiction, 36
creative skills
    as "creative muscle," 14–15
    focused freewriting, 19–22
    freewriting, characterized, 15–16
    freewriting, misconceptions
        about, 22–24
    freewriting, obstacles to, 18–19
    examples, 17–18, 21
    exercises, 17–18, 21–22
critical skills
    as "critical muscle," 14–15
    perfectionism, 25–28
    revision, 24–25

assignment, 28–29, 31
    examples, 29, 30–31
    exercise, 27
crowd-sourcing, 136

Daum, Meghan, 53
deductive argument structure, 144
deep writing, 160
detail, in personal essays, 69–70
dialogue, in personal essays, 67
direct quotation, 109

Elbow, Peter, 14, 193, 196
emotion, expressing, 74–76
emotional truth, 67
essay structure. *See* personal essays,
        structuring
essay writing
    creative skills, 14–24
    critical skills, 24–31
    genres of, 11–13
    revision, 13–14
    voice, 13, 24
    See also mindfulness; peer
        feedback; personal essays;
        research essays; texts,
        reading; texts, writing about
evidence-gathering, 89–91, 98
external awareness, 164–65

feedback. *See* peer feedback

Ferrante, Elena, 41

first-person pronouns, 143–44

five-paragraph essay structure, 54–57

focused freewriting, 19–22

formal close readings, 102

"frame" essay structure, 58

frameworks for interpretation, 89–90

freewriting
    characterized, 15–16
    for choosing topics, 45–47
    focused freewriting, 19–22
    mindfulness and, 160, 175–76
    misconceptions about, 22–24
    for personal essay structure, 49–50, 55–56
    potential obstacles to, 18–19
    prompts for responding to, 201–02
    for research essays, 134–35, 138–39
    for writing about texts, 91, 97–98, 103
    examples, 17–18, 21–22, 29
    exercises, 17–18, 21–22

genres, characterized, 11–13
    See also personal essays; research essays; texts, reading; texts, writing about

grammar and syntax, 197–98

headings, in research essays, 147

Herring, Laraine, 160, 173

human geography, 71

hypotheses, 132

imitation, in learning from others, 118

inductive argument structure, 144–46

informal essays, 28

information, verification of, 135–36

inner voices, 171–74

interpretation, of texts, 89–90

introductions, 108, 147–49

"I" pronoun in research essays, 143–44

Jamison, Leslie, 53–54

journal of noticings, 40–47

journal of questions, 129, 130

Lamott, Anne, 113

laziness, 127–28

learning from other writers, 116–21

librarians, 137

Lopate, Philip, 59, 68, 166

media types, 13

meditations, 12

mindfulness
    defined, 161–63
    external awareness, 164–65
    inner voices, 171–74
    internal mindfulness, 163–64
    our bodies and, 160
    overall benefits of, 158
    resistance to, 159, 165–68
    while writing, 170–71, 174–79
    examples, 173–74
    exercises, 162, 167

mini-essays, 28–29, 31

Morano, Michele, 53

Nhat Hanh, Thich, 167

nuance, 87–88

online sources, verification of, 135–36
organizing concept/object, 58–59
Orwell, George, 76
outlines, 62–63, 144–46

paragraphs, 147–51, 204
paraphrasing, 112–14
peer feedback
    defined, 182–84
    being a peer responder, 192–94
    fear of, 187
    framing feedback, 195–98
    general process, 198–200
    group dynamics, 204–05
    inadequacy and superiority, 185
    misconceptions about, 185–86
    problems with "tear it apart," 187–90
    prompts for responders, 201–04
    responding to feedback, 200
    for writings about texts, 120
    exercises, 184, 186
perfectionism, 25–28
personal close readings, 102
personal essays
    defined, 12, 36–38
    choosing topics, 40–47
    clichés, 38–40
    assignment, 43, 45–47
    examples, 35, 38, 41, 43–44
    exercise, 34
    See also personal essays, revising;
        personal essays, structuring
personal essays, revising
    conclusions, 76–78
    detail, 69–70
    dialogue, 67
    expressing emotion, 74–76

introducing yourself, 68–69
    place, 70–74
    planting a "seed," 65–66
    reading aloud, 78
    assignment, 78
    examples, 72, 73–74, 75–76
    exercises, 64, 67
personal essays, structuring
    five-paragraph structure, 54–57
    freewriting for, 49–50, 55–56
    outlines, 62–63
    published writers, structures
        used by, 53–54
    structural metaphors, 51–53
    templates for, 57–60
    working with structure, 60–62
    assignment, 63
    examples, 49, 59–60, 62–63
    exercise, 48
place, in personal essays, 70–74
plagiarism, 114–15
"précis" (formal close readings), 102
primary vs. secondary sources, 138
psychology and writing. See
        mindfulness

"question and answer" essay
        structure, 60
quotations, 98, 108–09

reading. See texts, reading
research essays
    anxieties around, 151–53
    boredom with, 128–29
    conclusions, 149–51
    finding sources, 135–38
    introductions, 147–49
    personal essays vs., 124–25

reading other essays, 132
refining topics, 130
research questions, 130–32
resistances to, 126–28
revising and finishing, 154–55
statements in, 142
structuring, 144–46
using "I" in, 143–44
working with source material,
    138–40
assignments, 133, 140, 153, 154
examples, 148–49, 150–53
exercises, 124, 134–35, 140, 146
revision
    critical muscle and, 24–25
    learning from other writers,
        116–21
    research essays, 154
    within writing process, 13–14
    See also personal essays, revising

Sanders, Scott Russell, 92
scaffolding, as structural metaphor,
    51–52
secret perfectionists, 26–27
sections, in research essays, 147–51
"seed" metaphor, 65–66
Sei Shōnagon, 75
Self, Will, 71
Smith, Zadie, 59–60
sound studies, 129
source material, 135–40
statements, in research essays, 142
structural metaphors, 50–53
structuring research essays, 144–46
    See also personal essays,
        structuring
summaries, writing, 109–12
syntax and grammar, 197–98

tastes, identifying, 119–20
"tear it apart," problems with,
    187–90
templates for personal essay
    structure, 57–60
texts, reading
    different ways of reading, 88
    gathering evidence, 90–91
    interpretation, 89–90
    to learn from other writers,
        116–20
    nuance, 87–88
    reading and re-reading, 82–86
    repetition in texts, 86–87
    assignments, 92–95, 96–99
    examples, 92, 94
    exercises, 83, 84
texts, writing about
    conclusions, 115
    finishing your essay, 121
    introductions, 108
    learning from other writers,
        116–20
    paraphrasing, 112–14
    plagiarism, 114–15
    quotation and citation, 108–09
    six-step process, 103–08
    thesis, defined, 100
    thesis-and-proof essays, 101–02,
        144
    writing summaries, 109–12
    assignments, 115, 120
    example, 113–14
    exercises, 112, 113, 118
theses, 51, 100, 104–07
    See also texts, writing about
thesis-and-proof essays, 101–02, 144
thread, as structural metaphor,
    51–53, 56, 65, 77

topics
    boredom with, 128–29
    for personal essays, 40–47
    refining, 130
truthful information, 136

voice
    defined, 13
    audience and, 50

    conversational, 28
    learning through imitation, 118
    maintaining consistency, 24
voices, inner, 171–74

Woolf, Virginia, 46, 72
working thesis, 104–07

From the Publisher

A name never says it all, but the word "Broadview" expresses a good deal
of the philosophy behind our company. We are open to a broad range of
academic approaches and political viewpoints. We pay attention to the
broad impact book publishing and book printing has in the wider world;
for some years now we have used 100% recycled paper for most titles.
Our publishing program is internationally oriented and broad-ranging.
Our individual titles often appeal to a broad readership too; many are
of interest as much to general readers as to academics and students.

Founded in 1985, Broadview remains a fully independent
company owned by its shareholders—not an imprint
or subsidiary of a larger multinational.

To order our books or obtain up-to-date information, please visit
broadviewpress.com.

broadview press
www.broadviewpress.com

This book is made of paper from well-managed FSC® - certified forests, recycled materials, and other controlled sources.